*Twayne's United States Authors Series*

Sylvia E. Bowman, *Editor*

INDIANA UNIVERSITY

*Louise Imogen Guiney*

# Louise Imogen Guiney

HENRY G. FAIRBANKS

*Saint Michael's College*

 **224**

Twayne Publishers, Inc.   ::   New York

writer's vocation, a prototype of the new "nun" emerging to serve society freely and professionally outside structured communities.

## ABOUT THE AUTHOR

Henry G. Fairbanks (Ph.D. University of Notre Dame), is Professor of Humanities at Saint Michael's College, Winooski, Vermont. He has served as curriculum chairman and, for fifteen years as chairman of the Humanities Department. Between 1947-50 he was founder and co-director of St. Michael's Playhouse—the first Equity company operating on the "star" system to take residence on an American campus as an integrated part of a college faculty. The theater is now in its twenty-fifth year of continuous operation. In 1959-60 he taught at the University of Saigon, Viet Nam, as a Smith-Mundt Fellow.

He is the author of *Louise Imogen Guiney: Laureate of the Lost,* and of her latest biographical sketch in the *New Catholic Encyclopedia.* He has also written *The Lasting Loneliness of Nathaniel Hawthorne,* a generalist's critique, and contributed articles to *PMLA, American Literature, College English, The Catholic World, America, The Commonweal, The University of Ottawa Review, Asian Studies,* besides numerous reviews and articles for journals of the day. During 1954-59 he was associate editor of the *Vermont Catholic Tribune* and presently is on the board of directors of the latter weekly, as well as a trustee and vice-president of Vermont Academy of Arts and Sciences.

# Preface

L OUISE Imogen Guiney's name is mostly forgotten today, and
all of the books which she published during her lifetime are
out of print, notwithstanding their number, generally high quality,
and rare *esprit*. A few lyrics (notably the martial ones: "The Knight
Errant," "Vigil-at-Arms," and "The Kings") and fewer personal
essays (such as "Reminiscences of a Fine Gentleman" and "On a
Preference for Living in England") still cling precariously to musty
anthologies. In one sense this neglect today is surprising because her
literary début in 1884 met the acclaim of Oliver Wendell Holmes,
Sr., the reigning autocrat of belles lettres in Boston's fading cultural
dominance. Even as late as 1940 Van Wyck Brooks retrospectively
considered her a phenomenon of singular radiance in the twilight
of New England's literary influence over America, calling her one of
the "compensatory gifts" of the rising Irish influence eroding the
citadel of Brahmin power.

In one sense, Miss Guiney partly acquiesced in the obscurity that
eventually overshadowed her; for she left America in 1900 for
the quiet of Oxford, dedicated to scholarly recovery of the merits of
bypassed talent, finding in lost Elizabethan and Caroline poets what
Sir Thomas Browne had called "the great meanings of minor things."
One work of estimable scholarship on which she had labored de-
votedly, *Recusant Poets,* was belatedly published in 1938–39, eighteen years after her death in 1920.

In another sense her obscurity was only partly self-elected inas-
much as she could neither accept nor resist the realism and naturalism
usurping the literary market in the swelling mainstream of an increasingly pragmatic, technology-oriented American society. She
tardily recognized the forces of change that had outmoded the
conventional poems for which the aging Holmes had acclaimed her,
and she underestimated the diminishing appeal of the personal
essay form for which she had undeniable gifts but which had always
assumed a leisurely readership no longer extant. She clung to traditional forms and to her own religious values, without failing, how-

ever, to recognize new talent or to encourage it by her impressively informed criticism. So she persisted in a light-but-learned humanism against the growing pressure of Germanic techniques and specialization being imported as the new models for university scholarship. Perhaps, with something of the stubbornness of her own favorite "Recusants," she refused to adapt simply in order to survive. But there was no bitterness in her widening isolation from the circles where her early brilliance had seemed to destine her for success.

She sustained a singular joy in the midst of routine and hardship. Both her industry and her versatility continued to attest a professional's absolute commitment to the vocation of writing. Nor was the harvest of her efforts negligible by any means, whether one assesses the early poetry which, in the 1880's, had made her something of a local laureate in Boston; the inextinguishable charm of her contributions to an already passé essay genre; the sparkle of her voluminous correspondence which affords insights into the literary absorptions and leading literati of her day; and the illuminating intuitions of the scholarship and editing which may well be her most enduring claim to attention. She lacked Emily Dickinson's innate genius as a poet and the elemental Dionysian impulse of Edna St. Vincent Millay's best lyrics; but in the interval between Dickinson and Millay hers was an authentically singing spirit that relieved the vapidity and conventionalism of most "lady"-verse effusions. As an essayist her best compositions rank with the finest of Agnes Repplier and Katherine Brégy, if Guiney does not actually surpass both in their field. As an epistolist among American ladies of letters, she is unique and invites comparison (beyond national borders) with the art of Lady Mary Wortley Montagu or Madame de Sévigné: sparkling, sophisticated yet intimate, and always the mirror of her age. As scholar-editor she eludes any offensive sex category and stands out as a person and an unchallengeable professional essentially.

In fact, her career "in making a go of it" in the male monopoly of professional letters anteceded the emancipation of suffrage or the agitations of today's "Women's Lib." Sociologically, her life also holds the mirror up to an American nativist past by reflecting the handicaps of membership in a subculture (Irish-immigrant and Catholic in her case) in a less tolerant society than today's. Neither experience (as woman or outsider) twisted her sanguine spirit toward the personal-confessional or toward the polemical-apologetic, though,

undoubtedly, each contributed toward her premature exhaustion.

Because her books are largely inaccessible and because her writings are indissociable from a true projection of her personality and her achievement, a biographical treatment seems dictated in the following chapters. These chapters, therefore, are intended to reflect the range of her works in the successive stages of her development: from the first pseudononymous poems to the posthumously published *Recusant Poets*. Quotation or paraphrase, designed to let her speak, may partly compensate for the difficulty in obtaining the original sources, as extracts from her letters that parallel the several phases of her career may capture something of her vital spirit. If, cumulatively, these chapters contribute to preserving the memory of Louise Imogen Guiney's gallant life and achievement, I will rest satisfied to have done for her what she spent her life in doing for so many authors, brushing time's dust, however briefly, from a name of neglected merit.

HENRY G. FAIRBANKS

*St. Michael's College*

# Acknowledgments

I wish to acknowledge, gratefully, the assistance of the following in completing this work: Miss Grace C. Guiney of Oxford, England, for her generosity in the instance of copyright permissions and of counsel; Reverend William L. Lucey, S.J., until his death Curator of the Guiney Collection at Holy Cross College, Worcester, Massachusetts, who shared his personal and library resources unstintingly and who collaborated in the periodical bibliography herein included; Mr. James M. Mahoney, Father Lucey's successor in office and spirit; Dr. Sylvia Bowman for her patience and indispensable guidance in preparing this edition; Mr. Joseph D. Sullivan, Assistant Director of the Durick Library Memorial Library, Saint Michael's College, Winooski, Vermont; Miss Mary Rivard, Reference Librarian, Saint Michael's College; the faculty and administration of Saint Michael's College for their facilitating research grant; the personnel of the Boston Public Library and of the Library of Congress for their courtesy and cooperation; Houghton Mifflin Company for permission to quote from *Happy Ending*; Sheed and Ward for permission to quote from *Recusant Poets*; Dr. Katherine E. McSweeney of Burlington, Vermont, for stimulating my interest in "L.I.G."; Reverend Francis Sweeney, S.J., of Boston College for sharing his knowledge of Guiney correspondence and friends; Mrs. Sandra M. Bourgea, secretary, for her expertise in decoding eccentric calligraphy; Katherine F. Fairbanks, my partner in this as in all else.

# Contents

# Chronology

Arnold's *Sohrab and Rustum;* "collector's find" of Henry Vaughan's *Thalia Rediviva* at Goodspeed's; takes position in Catalogue Room of Boston Public Library; *The Martyrs' Idyl and Shorter Poems.*

1900    Resigns from Boston Public Library.

1901    England, with Aunt Elizabeth Doyle; residence, Oxford; begins Vaughan researches; *Patrins* reissued.

1902    Edits Vaughan's *The Mount of Olives and Primitive Holiness;* aunt dies.

1904    *Robert Emmet: A Survey of His Rebellion and of His Romance; Hurrell Froude: Memoranda and Comments;* edits *Katherine Philips, "The Matchless Orinda."*

1906    Brief return to Boston to attend failing mother.

1907    Edits *Thomas Stanley: His Original Lyrics.*

1908    *Blessed Edmund Campion.*

1909–    Returns to Boston to mother's bedside; own deafness intensifies;

1910    *Happy Ending: The Collected Lyrics of Louise Imogen Guiney;* mother dies; Louise hospitalized; returns to England.

1911    Collaborates with Thomas Whittemore in editing *Post-Liminium: Essays and Critical Papers by Lionel Johnson.*

1912    Edits *Some Poems of Lionel Johnson, Newly Selected.*

1913    Begins *Recusant Poets* with the Reverend Geoffrey Bliss, S.J.

1914    *Blessed Edmund Campion* reissued.

1920    Dies, November 2, at Chipping Camden, Gloucestershire; buried in Wolvercote Cemetery, Oxford, beside aunt.

1927    Revised edition of *Happy Ending* posthumously published.

1938    Volume I, *Recusant Poets* posthumously published.

# Seed-Time

L OUISE Imogen Guiney was born in January, 1861, four months
before the Civil War began when President Lincoln was already
calling for recruits. She was correct, therefore, as well as characteristically whimsical, in recounting that, "Like the royal personages in
the drama, I was ushered on the stage of life, literally, with the
flourish of trumpets." The ideal of martial nobility, lodestar of her
life, was indelibly fixed by her earliest recollections recorded in "A
Day in Camp,"[1] where she spent, at age three, a day in the officers'
mess of her father's command, the Ninth Massachusetts, then strung
out along the Potomac. Innocent of the business of war, she was a
darling daughter of the regiment, toasted by the colonel's staff and
applauded by the soldiery.

The chivalric image was embodied in the person of General Robert
Patrick Guiney, brevetted for heroism at the age of twenty-eight. He
did disabuse her of the pageantry of war when wounds received in the
Wilderness campaign invalided him home, a shell-wracked figure for
the rest of his short life: "It was my earliest glimpse of the painful
side of war, when he stood worn, pale, drooping, waiting recognition
with a weary smile, at the door of the sunny house we all loved . . . .
What was this spectre with whom I must not frolic, on whose
shoulders I must not perch, whose head, bound in bandages, I must
not handle?"[2] The childish eyes that had delighted in colored
plates of the battles of Trafalgar and Austerlitz registered a darker
picture with shock.

### I  Father Image

But General Guiney's image never faded. He remained her
knight ideal, gallant in suffering as well as in battle, who moved
about the courts of law in Boston and was admired for his simplicity
and dignity. When Louise left home to attend the boarding school
conducted by the Madams of the Sacred Heart in Providence,[3]
she wrote her father letters that suggest a comradeship in arms, but
she sometimes addressed him as "Big Brother." At eleven, she

requested him to ask Santa Claus to bring her a little sword, "because we play soldiers here and I have a gun and a flag, and a sword is all I want." As late as 1876, when she was fifteen, she added in a postscript, "Please send my Scottish Chiefs."[4]

A year later, General Guiney, only forty-two, fulfilled her ideal of the knight by the way he died; for one of Louise's fixed principles was that "part of the business of life was to lose it handsomely."[5] Her father faced that end like the Chevalier de Bayard—eyes open, propped up against a tree. Almost at his doorstep, at the edge of Franklin Park Square, the wounded veteran felt a warning spurt of blood to his lips. With instinctive composure, he removed his hat, knelt and crossed himself, supporting himself against a tree. So he was found—so Louise remembered him.

Years later she told his story in an article for his alma mater, printed in *The Holy Cross Purple* (June, 1896); and still later in a biographical sketch, "Guiney, Patrick Robert," in the *Catholic Encyclopedia* (Vol. VII, 1910). Both accounts retold an immigrant saga familiar to Americans: her father had come from Tipperary to Maine, in 1839; from factory wheel-boy to college student; from law studies at an old judge's elbow in Portland to admission to the Maine bar; from private to brigadier general; from editor to assistant district attorney. In a larger sense, Louise was writing his story when she wrote biographies of Henri du Verger, Comte de la Rochejaquelin, of Robert Emmet, or of that civilian, but no less "dear and battling spirit,"[6] William Hazlitt. Certainly her most anthologized lyrics mirror her father's soldier's features: "The Knight Errant," "Vigil-at-Arms," and the lament for vanished heroes which she penned on the flyleaf of her copy of Clarendon's *History of the Rebellion.*

> How life hath cheapened, and how blank
> The Worlde is! like a fen
> Where long ago unstained sank
> The starrie gentlemen:
> Since Marston Moor and Newbury drank
> King Charles his gentlemen.[7]

Along with her ardent Catholic faith, General Guiney was the shaping force in Louise's life. During her residence in Auburndale with her mother after General Guiney's death in 1877, she kept his

sword, spurs, and regimental scarf mounted on the wall of her study beside the flag which had draped his coffin. These memorabilia, treasured throughout her life, she bequeathed with her own voluminous writings to form the Guiney Collection at the College of the Holy Cross in Worcester, Massachusetts.

Perhaps, in addition to the inspiration which he supplied to her code of noblesse oblige and her characteristic themes, he had some share in her predilection for letters. As a young man in Maine, he had been subeditor of the *Lewiston Advocate* and, subsequently, became a regular contributor to the *Boston Times*. For a man of action who had seen service in thirty-two engagements and who bore the testament of numerous wounds, he was a bookish man who took pride in his daughter's talents.

Her own pride in a fighting Irish ancestry (great-granddaughter and granddaughter of sires who had been out in "the forty-five and again in "the ninety-eight") made her a natural genealogist whose development solidified her later achievements as an editor and as a scholar. This innate aptitude, sharpened on hero worship of her father and honed by a sense of duty to the immigrant Irish among whom he was a leader, was refined to a keener edge by the self-conscious superiority of the dominant Yankees who had accepted her personally but who literally held the field in New England. She staked out a claim, romantically, to wider fields of heraldry which fructified years afterward in England in research done at the Bodleian Library.

Her conception of nobility, however, was excellence, not pedigree, as she explained in her 1888 essay on "The Ethics of Descent": "The truth is, we belong, from the beginning, to many masters, and are unspeakably beholden to the forming hands of the phenomena of the universe, rather than to the ties of blood. What really makes one live, gives him his charter of rights . . . is, often enough, no human agency at all . . . . Far from being the domestic product we take ourselves to be, we are strangely begotten of the unacknowledged . . . and owe the thing we are to the most trivial thing we touch. We are poor relations of every conceivable circumstance."[8]

Less speculation is needed to connect the general's influence with her growth into one of America's better elegiasts, for war and death are indissociable. By vitue of his military prestige among the Boston Irish, and by Irish prominence itself in the ranks and officer

corps of the Union Army, Louise, the general's poet-daughter, could hardly avoid a quasi-official role as the local laureate to "the Boys in Blue." When she complied, she turned out unforced occasional pieces like her odes to General Grant and General Sherman—the latter, a particularly fine handling of the exacting Horatian model. Happily, she eluded this perilous type-casting by eschewing any kind of public role. Her typical elegies were not flowery Memorial Day effusions, although one of the best remembered is, indeed, entitled "Memorial Day" and begins "O Day of roses and regret" and ends "Hail, dearest few! and soon, alas, Farewell."[9]

But most of her elegies, from the mid-1880's until World War I, were spontaneous responses to the loss of any promise prematurely extinguished. Their range was extensive: from lament for Jacobite cavaliers, loyal to a doomed cause, to the classically Greek epitaphs of the "Alexandriana," which duped some Boston professors into acclaiming them superb translations of ancient originals; to her grief for the young Oxonians deserting their quadrangles for the trenches of Flanders ("The golden English heads like harvest grain"[10]); to her unexcelled tribute to the St. Bernard dog most cherished among her many favorites of his breed.

> But thou, instead, hast found
> The sunless April uplands underground,
> And still, wherever thou art, I must be.
> My beautiful! arise in might and mirth,
> (For we were tameless travellers from our birth);
> Arise against thy narrow door of earth,
> And keep the watch for me.[11]

Some critics have reduced the relationship between General Guiney and Louise to neat Freudian formula: father fixation. Because his influence was so dominant, in contrast to that exercised by her mother; because she never married; because her religious ideals were so high as to suggest "the natural nun"—a pattern seems to emerge. One scholar has made this father fixation his thesis[12]; but to accept it unqualified is to overlook the degree to which her feudal nature was permeated with the concept of *comitatus*. Duty and fidelity were the roots of her being. Of these, her father was one memorable personification.

## II  *Mother and Daughter*

Admittedly, her mother hardly figures in Louise's works, save in the voluminous correspondence, where references amply testify to a genuinely filial bond. Louise, only sixteen when her father died, continued to live with Mrs. Guiney in America for the next twenty-three years; and she often assumed the major responsibility of supporting the widow reduced to living off a veteran's pension. This sense of duty largely explains Louise's acquiescence to the necessity of finding employment, first in the Auburndale Post Office and, afterward, in the Catalogue Room of the Boston Public Library, although both positions wrenched her from preoccupation with literature.

Mother and daughter traveled to England and Ireland in each other's company. Mrs. Guiney joined Louise in England when the younger woman, now determined to renew her commitment to letters, had left America in 1901 for permanent residence abroad. When Mrs. Guiney returned alone in 1903, hers was a normal nostalgia for the security of the familiar. Yet Louise recrossed the Atlantic in 1906 to visit her; and she returned in 1909 on news of the mother's illness to remain with her until her death the following year.

There was, however, a suppressed tension in their relationship. Mrs. Guiney, basically, was a conventional Victorian matriarch who was governed primarily by "common sense." Louise, a free spirit, was capable of unworldly dedication incomprehensible to ordinary standards. Mrs. Guiney was proud of her daughter's literary reputation, but, for the wrong reasons, as Louise admitted once in a letter to the Reverend William H. Van Allen: "She cares for me today, not as my Aunt Betty did, all her lonely life, for myself; but for my exterior prowess, for whatever stir I can make; her affection varies just as I feed, or do not feed, her pride in me."[13]

In May, 1910, after her mother's death and her own return to England, Louise published a verse memorial in *McClure's*. The title, *"De Amore Amicorum,"* seemed rather distant as an expression of filial grief, and more an expression of gratitude to the friends who had honored the funeral of Mrs. Guiney and sustained Louise in her bereavement. It was characteristic of Louise, however, to universalize pain by suppressing any personal identification bordering on self-pity or sentimentality. Moreover, considering

her understanding of the doctrine of the Communion of Saints and
her sympathy with St. Augustine's apparent coldness in alluding
to his dead Monica as "fellow citizen in heaven," Louise's "Love of
Friends" was not incompatible with profound feeling:

> Heaped on one unworthy heart
> Balm which never ends;
> Dead, I shall inhale it yet,
> (Ah, verbena, mignonette!)
> Precious Love-of-Friends.[14]

### III  *Spinster*

That Louise remained single throughout her fifty-nine years
is more explicable by her dedication to letters, which even Mrs.
Guiney could not fully appreciate, than by automatic Freudian interpretation. She was absolutely normal in her relations with both men
and women, moving freely between the sexes, warmly spontaneous
and affectionate. She knew, without feminine assertiveness, that she
was a natural peer of male professional associates; but she understood, patiently, that the unformulated rules of society had decreed
an unequal distribution of rewards along mythical sexual lines. She
sympathized with contemporary suffragettes, but her innate repugnance to anything fanatical withheld her endorsement of public antics.
Of course, she enjoyed a special liberation from their gnawing in-
feriority because of her personal acceptance in the more democratic
republic of letters. She could, accordingly, admit to Richard
Watson Gilder in a letter of August 7, 1894, that "I am not in the
least given to any violent interest in womankind, however, such as
has addled the country's brains of late. Give me a manandwoman
world: 'tis good enough!"[15]

Nor is there any evidence of her failure to respond to masculine
appeal. Her best, and most frequent, correspondents were men. Her
disposition toward some of them was affectingly flirtatious, notably
in the instance of Fred Holland Day, to whom she wrote hundreds
of letters deposited by the terms of Day's will in the archives of the
Library of Congress. The legend of "Louise, the Nun" derives from
the tenuous speculations of Eva Mabel Tenison's generally admirable
biography of 1923.[16] It received currency, then and afterward,
because of Guiney's devout life and the genuine spirituality of her

religious lyrics. It was compounded by the pietistic incapacity of most pre-Vatican II readers to reconcile ardent faith with secular involvement, a view no longer tenable by virtue of contemporary church emphasis on personal freedom and social activism.

## IV *Vocation*

For Louise, however, "the life of perfection" never excluded worldly commitment as her admired Jesuits professed it: "For the Greater Honor and Glory of God."[17] She needed a broad margin to her life to express the richness of her spirit. Neither Jansenist-Catholic nor Hibernian-Puritan, she harbored no specter of *contemptus mundi*. Indeed, she attended rehearsals of her own adaptations of French plays: she promoted the vogue of Aubrey Beardsley; and she loathed the stuffiness of Victoria and Albert and longed for the gusto of Nell Gwynne. She preserved, nonetheless, a nun's integrity, and she surpassed a nun's sacrifice in her self-abnegation to fulfill her calling as a writer.

When pain, want, and the inevitable attrition of hope multiplied with the passing years, she took increasing solace from the resources of religion. In one rare confessional sonnet, "Astraea," she explained her withdrawal from early literary ambitions and the excitement of literary cliques—but only as renunciation of one good for a better, never as repudiation:

> Since I avail no more, O men! with you,
> I will go back unto the gods content;
> For they recall me, long with earth inblent,
> Lest lack of faith divinity undo.
> I served you truly while I dreamed you true,
> And golden pains with sovereign pleasure spent:
> But now, farewell! I take my sad ascent,
> With failure over all I nursed and knew.
> Are ye unwise, who would not let me love you?
> Or must too bold desires be quieted?
> Only to ease you, never to reprove you,
> I will go back to heaven with heart unfed:
> Yet sisterly I turn, I bend above you,
> To kiss (ah, with what sorrow!) all my dead.[18]

The opening stanza of *"Deo Optimo Maximo"* retells the struggle between temporal and eternal and of her growing election of the latter.

But, again, the transient is honored as sacramental; only union with God is sacrament:

> All else for use, One only for desire;
> Thanksgiving for the good, but thirst for Thee:
> Up from the best, whereof no man need tire,
> Impel Thou me.[19]

Louise's character was composed of self-denials, not denials. "Thanksgiving for the Good," deeply implanted in her being, made her a quintessentially joyful poet. The vitality in her best lyrics led Katherine Brégy to call her a "Christian Valkyrie."[20] Louise herself would have grasped John Milton's indictment in *Areopagitica* of "fugitive and cloistered virtue." She was no nun strayed from the convent, longing for readmission; but sisterlike, she extended the charity of religious love to a catholic, if more vulnerable, community encompassing human brotherhood.

## V   *Elmhurst*

Nuns, unquestionably, had a lasting influence on Louise Guiney. They not only deepened her Catholic cultural heritage but strengthened her predisposition to the heroic *gesta* of "long ago and far away." For the Religious of the Sacred Heart who undertook her education from the age of eleven until her graduation at seventeen, were royalist *émigrées* from France. Founded in the aftermath of the French Revolution to serve the needs of well-to-do daughters of the nobility and *haute-bourgeoisie,* the "Madams" of the Sacred Heart had established a finishing school for young ladies-to-be in Providence, Rhode Island, comparable to their older foundations in New Orleans and in New York. Under their gentle tutelage, American girls of means, of all faiths, enrolled at Elmhurst Academy to acquire refinement, domestic management, languages, and music before making their début into society. While hoyden Louise had some difficulty in adjusting to this formal regimen (especially to mathematics and sewing), she drank in the exiles' vivid recollections of an *ancien régime* which rarely ceased to be the real present to them and to their rapt auditor. Was not the Comtesse de Grammont, one of their founding patronesses, a *dame d'honneur* at the court of Marie Antoinette? Did they not know all the details of the *Résist-*

*ance* to godlessness and republicanism in the wild *Vendée*? Louise, who preferred playing soldier to all else, was an apt pupil for their creed of "throne-and-altar."

Elmhurst, which had the seclusion and grandeur of a manor on the outskirts of the city, was surrounded by orchards and fields and was approached by the winding avenue of arched trees from which it took its name. Formerly the old Grosvenor estate, it was a home away from home where the nuns gave love, as well as sound instruction, to their few dozen charges. But, at first, liberty-loving Louise resented her enrollment. Her recalcitrance had less to do with the school or its teachers than with her instinctive opposition to authority. Her first days in private school in Boston had elicited the same rebelliousness; then hardly five, she had shown herself the stubborn daughter of a fighting general:

> I did not like the looks of the teacher; I disliked the room. I looked the children over, and made up my mind that I did not like them either, . . . I remember that the teacher tried to make me take part . . . , but I was mute; the sphinx herself was not more obstinately dumb than I was.
>
> I made no demonstration at home, but waited until next morning when preparations were made to send me to school again. Then I quietly informed them that I was not going anymore . . . . I did not cry: I simply stood still and refused to budge. I only yielded to superior force, for my mother took my head and the nurse my heels, and I was ignominiously lugged to school. . . . As fast as they put me in the room, I dashed out; and finally I was tied in my chair. That was the way I went to school every day, until convinced that I was conquered.[21]

Although some few years had intervened since her childish rebellion when Mrs. Guiney conducted her, in August, 1872, to registration at Elmhurst, the old academic aversion persisted. To comfort herself against the prospects of immurement in a convent school, Louise had carried her "best blue gun, and a collection of agate marbles." But one young nun on the staff, Mother Samuella Shaw, converted Louise when she outstripped her in a mad race through the apple orchard and cleared box hedges in a graceful leap where thin-legged Louise hesitated to follow. Reviewing her introduction to Elmhurst, alumna Louise admitted that the leap had settled it: "I judged everything by its capacity to run, jump, and swim. She didn't know that; but she broke down, by that one flight in air, all my objections to a contemplative life."[22]

Her changed views toward Elmhurst are confirmed in a letter which she sent to her father in May, 1874, one of those monthly exchanges which, even from the earliest childish ones, communicate the unmistakable ring of the distinguished epistolist-to-be:

You can't imagine how delighted I am to hear you are coming in early June. Will you try and be here on the very first day? . . . I often wonder if Elmhurst wasn't the garden of Eden once, it is so lovely . . . Hattie and I were sitting on the hill, overlooking the brook—idly throwing pebbles in the rippling water, and discussing the beauties of Nature, this morning, and really how one can say they dislike this place, is a puzzle to me. The sky is azure blue, with feathery clouds resting like shadows on the soft surface. The lake looked so clear and sandy and the birds singing in the trees made the place so enchanting. So we sat down and staid a long time, thinking how Bella Wilson could stick up for Canada (the Sacred Heart Convent there) or the grounds there, when she sees our lovely treasure. Even the little frogs seemed to enjoy the pure air, for one of these green animals popped up his head, winked his eye in a froggish way, as much as to say, "Nice, isn't it?" The young rogue![23]

In an earlier letter she had noted that she was improving in English, which seemed to be her "greatest talent," along with music. ("I know Mamma would like to hear of my improvement in prudence," she added.) Mamma might well suspect that prudence was not Louise's forte, for classmates regularly elected her "President of the Games" from enrollment until graduation by virtue of her imagination and audacity. But General Guiney must have chuckled with admiration at the pluck which Louise showed in badgering a muskrat into his den and trying to haul him out by his tail. "I know all their habits," she confided, "and some fine day I will follow up my adventure by penetrating to his hole. I will be very kind to him, as he has won my respect by his courage."[24] If few classmates were as knowledgeable about muskrats, they, too, recognized a born writer in Louise. They made her editor-in-chief of *The Signet,* the school magazine; and, in the senior class prophecy, they foresaw her destiny as renown in literature, hedging the vision with "unless she chooses to become a missionary—to the Indians!"

The prophesied writer's career was soon vindicated with more accuracy than confirms the predictions of most commencement day seers. *Songs at the Start* (1884) was in print only five years after

graduation, and it contains a reference to class plays at Elmhurst which none of her schoolmates could miss:

> *Private Theatricals*
>
> You were a haughty beauty, Polly,
>> (That was in the play,)
> I was the lover melancholy;
>> (That was in the play.)
> And when your fan and you receded,
> And all my passion lay unheeded,
> If still with tender words I pleaded,
>> That was in the play!
>
> I met my rival at the gateway,
>> (That was in the play,)
> And so we fought a duel straightway;
>> (That was in the play.)
> But when Jack hurt my arm unduly,
> And you rushed over, softened newly,
> And kissed me, Polly! truly, truly,
>> Was that in the play?[25]

Both *Songs at the Start* and her next published volume of poems, *The White Sail* (1887), also showed that she had not forgotten other theatricals at Elmhurst. Both refight the French Revolution and glorify the defeated royalist cause in "A Ballad of Metz," "À Chouan," "Moustache," and "Vergniaud in the Tumbril." And *Monsieur Henri,* a galloping little biography of the hero of the Vendéan Resistance, was dedicated to Mother Marie-Ange Bondroit, R.S.C.J., "as a little token of an honorable and life-long debt."

But the really enduring debt was neither girlish dreams of blue-blooded heroes nor legends of a golden age when throne and altar were united. Time leveled these, like the *bocage* in far-off Vendée, to due proportions. What endured, like the memory of her father, was the foundation of a happy childhood, where ideals were established in love past erosion by the disappointments and sufferings ahead. By 1907, when Louise contributed "Memories of an Old Girl" to the April reunion of Elmhurst alumnae, she had experienced enough of life to appreciate the essence and extent of the debt. "Memories" touched on many things in grateful inventory, but lingered longest at the chapel door: "the first little chapel, with the windows always

open, and the fragrance of a thousand flowers within and without, where so many of us made our First Communions, and got our grip for life on supernatural things, 'the things that are most excellent.'"

Of course, she acquired other accomplishments under the care of the sisters: the command of French that served her well, subsequently, as translator and scholar; the knowledge of music that she chose to list among her qualifications for work at the Boston Public Library when she made no mention of her numerous publications; and the solid grounding in history and literature which led Smith College to offer her a position on the faculty until informed that she held no formal degree.[26]

For Elmhurst, like other finishing schools for young ladies at the time, had done its task well. Such institutions had assumed the burden of educating American womanhood before many colleges had opened their doors to co-education. William Dean Howells observed the result, ruefully, in the superior girls crowding the verandas of summer resorts: "altogether brighter and quicker than the young men they meet."[27] Perhaps Elmhurst was among the best of these finishing schools; for Louise, at least, could step from the day of graduation with quiet assurance into a literary world dominated by men. It was no fault of her teachers that she had been prepared for life, not for making a living. That was their purpose. That was her parents' wish.

But General Guiney had died two years before her graduation. In leaving her "more glory than dollars," he was still shaping her life.[28]

# Firstlings

THE years following Elmhurst were spent in the village of Auburndale, a few miles from Boston, where the Guineys, accompanied by Aunt Betty and a menagerie of dogs and cats, had moved from increasingly unfashionable Roxbury. Their new home was a more fortunate choice than Silas Lapham's, who had also moved out of the South End for similar reasons. Auburndale then was an idyllic place and time for Louise—a Horton almost, where she continued to prepare for the future after Milton's leisurely model. No doubt the class prophecy, its levity notwithstanding, confirmed the self-appraisal of her "greatest talent" reported to her father. Soon she was writing, and almost as soon, she was publishing, under a *nom de plume,* poems in the *Pilot,* the Boston *Evening Transcript,* the New York *Home Journal,* and the New York *Tribune.*

Until recently critics have dated her first poems from 1884, with the publication of *Songs at the Start* and they have understandably identified *A Roadside Harp* (1893) as her first collection. Actually, *Songs at the Start,* which won the applause of Oliver Wendell Holmes, Sr., on its appearance, was itself a collection, in good part, of poems already in circulation since 1880. The Norton-Guiney letters at Holy Cross establish the earlier beginnings past doubt;[1] for Rachel Norton, to whom most of the 234 letters were sent, was Louise's closest confidante in these years, as well as a life-long correspondent.[2] Not only do these letters fill in early gaps in the published *Letters,* but they also include journal clippings of Louise's first efforts which were preserved by the admiring friend who knew about her penname.

This *nom de plume* alternated between "P.O.L." ("Poor Ole Louise," or "Polly" of her "Private Theatricals"?) and "Roger Holden," a combination of paternal and maternal genealogies: Sir Roger de Gyney of Norfolk, and the Lancastershire Holdens.[3] The two constant companions must have relished the secret shared. Certainly, in their frequent walks together along the Charles River, escorted by Louise's St. Bernards, they had occasion to giggle at the

discomfiture caused Thomas Bailey Aldrich, editor of the *Atlantic Monthly,* by a playful hoax perpetrated by Louise in 1881. She had sent the *Transcript* an unsigned poem entitled "Two Idols" which aped Thomas Aldrich's style and vapid sentiment, and the *Transcript* had printed it with credits to the well-known "T.B.A." Bailey's furtive acknowledgment of authorship, with flustered expostulations of forgetfulness as to composition or mailing, set Bostonian sophisticates tittering at his implications of inspiration and timelessness.

## I  *Patron*

A third person was also party to the identity of "P.O.L."—John Boyle O'Reilly, strenuous editor of the *Pilot.* O'Reilly, whom Van Wyck Brooks had paired with Louise as Hibernian compensation for the Irish invasion of Boston, had captured the city's imagination by his exploits as Fenian fighter, his daring escape on a whaler from an Australian penal colony, and his vigorous molding of the *Pilot* into a paper of influence. He had been a close friend of General Guiney, and he became a patron of the dead general's daughter. He had published "P.O.L.'s" first printed poem—"Charles Sumner" (December 11, 1880), beginning "It is November: yet I feel the breath / Of breezes round me that are born in spring"—and he had printed at least twenty-two more of her poems before *Songs at the Start* went to press. Long before its release, Louise had dropped the subterfuge and had begun using the now familiar "L.I.G." as her signature.

But O'Reilly had done more than open his columns to her submissions; he had used his own prestige to introduce her at nineteen to Boston literary circles that included Francis Parkman, Brooks Adams, George Parsons Lathrop, and James and Annie Fields. When *Songs at the Start* made its formal début in 1884 (properly dedicated to him), he personally contributed the *Pilot's* review, singling out "A Ballad of Metz" for special praise because it matched Robert Browning "in its strength of expression and vigorous movement."[4] Bostonians agreed, generally, that a new talent had risen in their midst capable of appreciating their glories; for *Songs at the Start* featured poems about the Hall of Flags in the State House and King's Chapel on Tremont Street, besides two apostrophes to the historic Charles River.

Nor was O'Reilly's recognition of the Browningesque vigor extravagantly biased. Louise's innate martial *esprit* predisposed her to swinging cadences that irresistibly summoned memories of Browning's "How They Brought the Good News from Ghent to Aix." Although her virtuosity in handling the anapest had to wait a few years for perfection in "The Wild Ride,"[5] something of genuine force, responding sensitively to the elemental and the untamed, marks "Gloucester Harbor" even in *Songs at the Start:*

> The brown ruddy children that fear not,
> Lean over the quay, and they hear not
>    Warning of lips;
> For their hearts go a-sailing, a-sailing,
> Out from the wharves and the wailing
>    After the ships.
>
> On to the central Atlantic,
> Where passionate, hurrying, frantic
>    Elements meet;
> To the play and the calm and commotion
> Of the treacherous, glorious ocean,
>    Cruel and sweet.

Tennyson, too, received the flattery of novice imitation in *Songs at the Start,* conspicuously in "The Sea Gull." But Louise, intrinsically incapable of a spiritless line, became no mere carbon copy of the most admired mentor. Some of the lines—"High as a dream thou art!" and "Beautiful is thy coming"—are genuine Guiney.

> Over the ships that are anchored
>    Over the fleets that part,
> Over the cities dark by the shore,
>    High as a dream thou art!
>
> Beautiful is thy coming,
>    Light is thy wing as it goes:
> And O! but to leap and follow this hour
>    Thy perfect flight to the close.
>
> O but to leap and follow
>    Where freedom and rest may be;
> Where the soul that I loved in surpassing love
>    Hath vanished away with thee!

An authentic Cavalier note also rings in the stirrup-cup toast of "A Jacobite Revival"; "Here's to the proud, forgotten names,/ Here's to the Stuart, Charles and James!" Vitality also pulsates in meter and message of the dramatic ballad, "Charondas, the Greek": "But who comes armed to the public hall/Shall suffer his death before us all." At publication, "Charondas" automatically inherited an audience captive to the declamatory recitative. To it, however, Louise brought an inner irony more congenial to modern taste: the tension inherent between soldier and citizen virtue, and the right priority of the latter. For Charondas, the councillor who had decreed the separation of sword and senate, killed himself to uphold the law when, too hastily returning from battle to announce victory, he became the first to break it:

> "I seal the law with my soul and might:
>    I do not break it," Charondas said.
> He raised his blade, and plunged to the hilt,
> Ah! vain their rush, for in glory and guilt,
>    He lay on the marble, dead.

Its austere republican hero and its fulsome rhetoric look dated now; but, in its time, it was no mean example of the elocutionary diet then served by schoolboy orators at patriotic feasts. Moreover, like all the other poems in *Songs at the Start,* it was excluded by Louise from subsequent collections.[6] More importantly, it evolved into a worthier successor—the classic perfection of "Tarpeia."

The elegiac note, which was to evolve into one of her distinctive achievements in the years ahead, is embryonic in *Songs at the Start.* Most typical of the genre is "The Neighbor," a rare tribute from a young Celt to a Puritan ancient,[7] which has the freshness and simplicity characterizing the volume generally. Its ten-line, couplet stanzas artfully adjust to the meditative scene and its intimate address to the occupant of the grave before which the poet stands in a quiet corner of King's Chapel burial ground. Loss is universalized; the fraternity of young and old becomes a genuine communion of saints; and the poem ends, apologetically, on a note of irrepressible joy, confessing the poet's compulsive youth and the hope of general resurrection:

> Who art thou that nigh to me
> Alone doth dwell, perpetually?

The latch against thy door is mute,
I have not heard thy kind salute,
  . . . . . . . . .

Ah, neighbor mine, unneighborly!
  . . . . . . . . .

My silent neighbor! thou and I
Keep unobtrusive company.
  . . . . . . . . .

And March by March the robin sings,
Against the solemn porch of King's,
His sweet good morrow to us both.
O be not harsh with me, nor wroth,
That I, apart from all the throng,
Break, too, thy silence with a song!

The sympathy for the lost that aches throughout the poems of the years ahead and that prompts the sustained rescue missions of her scholarship, is represented in *Songs at the Start* by "Crazy Margaret" (Shades of Wordsworth's "Idiot Boy"!) and by that strange sonnet entitled "Criminal, 1865." John Wilkes Booth, assassin of Lincoln, might seem an unlikely subject for one with Louise's personal investment in the Civil War; for her treatment has none of the maledictory of a Northern psalm. But her partisanship was always with the lost, and it was guaranteed if such individuals possessed the saving grace of some genius and much courage. To Louise Guiney, waste of spirit was the tragedy, not failure.

All told, *Songs at the Start* was an auspicious beginning. Her seminal themes were there, to be mined and refined throughout the rest of her life, with some attendant loss of simplicity as her style becomes more cryptic and elliptical and her themes allusively erudite and self-consciously literary. While uneven, the execution of these first showed unmistakable promise and, occasionally, flashes of brilliance. The hand of her guiding masters may show too openly: Browning in "A Ballad of Metz," Tennyson in "The Sea Gull," Wordsworth in "Boston, From the Bridge"; but, patently, Louise had learned their lessons well. She was only twenty-three and in print, but it would take her many more years to grasp the grim truth of the lines which she had had Chaucer speak in one of the best Petrarchan sonnets of her maiden volume:

Child! this is the earth-completing Paradise,
And thou, that strayest here, art centuries dead.[8]

# Harvest

*SONGS at the Start* not only won plaudits for Louise, but unlocked editors' doors and plunged her into the whirl of literary sets. *Harper's,* which promptly reprinted its six stanzas on "Brook Farm," staggered her with the honorarium of twenty dollars. Within three months of the first review of *Songs,* the *Atlantic* featured her article on Leigh Hunt ("An English Literary Cousin"),[1] the first of many thereafter accepted by the influential monthly. The City of Boston commissioned her to write a memorial ode on the recently deceased General Grant,[2] and the honorarium was truly astounding—one hundred dollars!

Typical of Louise, the commission was "distressing" because, though she was always in need and although she readily complied, she felt guilty about profiting from the deeds of heroes and was reluctant to produce under pressure. The memorial ode was applauded, and she was dubbed "soldierhood's most ardent minstrel"; but, privately, she confided to Rachel Norton that, in pocketing "the ill-gotten gains," she would fall many pegs in her own estimation.[3] A quaint feudal repugnance to money-changing, fixed in almost *hidalgo* principles, kept her naïve in money matters. Indeed, a friend of this period, Alice Brown, observed that Louise would "not cross the street to advance her own interests";[4] but she would cross the ocean to restore Henry Vaughan's grave or Clarence Mangan's reputation. Nevertheless, the seventy-five dollars in royalties netted from *Songs at the Start* was realistically welcomed, for Louise had "to pay tithes, you know, and contribute to the support of the family," as she explained to Rachel Norton.[5]

Always a stern critic of her own work, Louise had no illusions about their merits. Her manuscripts testify to constant revision after, as well as before, publication. She was not just bantering when she called her firstlings "little odds and ends, or windfalls."[6] She proved her sincerity by excluding them all from any subsequent collections, even that little gem of *vers de société,* "Private Theatricals."

However, as a young woman of twenty-three, she thoroughly en-

joyed the social whirl following her début, especially the tour of New York in the company of Richard Watson Gilder, editor of *Century;* conversations with Gotham literati gathering at Gilder's home; introduction to Helen Gray Cone, author of *The Ride to the Lady* and *Oberon and Puck* ("Emma Lazarus was asked to come, but has a sick father"); plays at *Wallack's*; concerts at the *Musée;* "a leg show at the Bijou"; and Sunday Mass off Madison Avenue with "the most *toney* Papistical" congregation imaginable ("nobody but Beauty, Wealth, and Culture, I'm afraid, has much business there").[7]

## I  *Essayist*

But Louise's place was back in Boston where those "family tithes" had to be paid. First came a volume of essays, *Goose-Quill Papers* (1885); then her second collection of poetry, *The White Sail and Other Poems* (1887), with more articles to *Atlantic, Lippincott's, Catholic World,* and *Wide Awake* intervening.

*Goose-Quill Papers* was not her first prose publication, for she published in *Atlantic* an article on Leigh Hunt in October, 1884; and her first-known publication in prose had appeared in the Boston *Sunday Budget* almost two years earlier on January 8, 1882— a girlishly saccharine story entitled "The Romance of a Postman."[8] There it had won second prize of thirty dollars, though in itself (and quite patently to Louise), it was no prize—award notwithstanding. She had limited talent for fiction, and less for dialogue, as *Lovers' Saint Ruth's and Other Tales* (1895) and *The Secret of Fougereuse* (1898) would subsequently confirm.

On the other hand, she was a "natural" as a writer of the essay. *Goose-Quill Papers,* charmingly inscribed to Oliver Wendell Holmes, Sr., has more to reveal about her future development than the seminal *Songs at the Start.* Nevertheless, she could honestly admit to a Boston "blue-stocking" friend, even before its publication: "My new little book promises to be fair to see, though I won't answer for its irresponsible and 'court-jesterish' contents."[9] Looking back on it critically, she called it "very anserine," indeed.[10] Many years later, anticipating the English cold, she firmly repeated her estimate: "*Goosequill Papers* would be capital to light fires with next winter."[11]

She was partly right. The virtue in the collection was its style, not its substance. Whimsicality was a nosegay for a day, not a deeply

rooted plant. Holmes received not only the complimentary dedication but the flattery of presumptuous imitation. For one so young,
however exquisitely fluent or picturesquely learned, the role of mini-
autocrat was usurpation. The essays were warmed-over recipes culled
from Charles Lamb and Sir Thomas Browne. The titles were too
coy; the development, too precious. The allusions presumed an Ar-
cadian community of bibliophiles where books were the staple
diet and curiosa, the dessert. The essays looked back, beyond
Holmes, to schoolgirl prolusions in *The Signet* at Elmhurst; and,
beyond that unworldly circle, they appealed to a readership already
passé. By 1885, the leisurely personal essay (for which she was an
adept by temperament and training) had been mangled mortally beneath the steam-age juggernaut.

Some of the inclusions have autobiographical importance,
notably "A Child in Camp"; "Mathematics," which humorously
accounts for her inbred aversion to the Black Art; and "Vagabondiana," which asserts her love of untrammeled liberty. Some
of Vagabondiana's lines cling to the memory: "The vagabond
is a modern representative of the knight errant . . . Everybody's
property is his in fief. . . . There is that in his eye which awes
the merchantman, and mesmerizes the maid at the hostel gate."
Nevertheless, the mintage of her aphorisms is counterfeit; and
Katherine Brégy is right in her reluctant concession that these
essays "are perhaps the only things she ever wrote that could not
acquit themselves of a slight pedantry."[12] Significantly, Louise
twelve years later preserved only two essays from *Goose-Quill
Papers* for reprinting in *Patrins:* "An Open Letter to the
Moon" and "On Teaching One's Grandmother How to Suck Eggs."
Even so, these essays look callow among the mature essays composed in the interval.

Yet *Goose-Quill Papers* is important in her development. Lightness and learning are there, if too airily; and the stylist is undeniably
present. Already evident are the critical principles and philosophy
that remained constant during her life, and which she elaborated in
*Patrins,* especially in the long *"Inquirendo"* on Charles II, "Wilful Sadness in Literature," and "The Harmless *versus* the Rabid
Scholar." A fairly random selection suffices for illustration:[13]

I resent the doctrine of absorption into the restful bosom of Brahma. An'
it please you, I aspire to Mars.

Life is a breathing-space between two eternities, a holiday with appalling realities behind and before.

We die and are forgotten; but must we forget?

The mind is fearless as long as there is no reproach of conscience. When that comes, come breakage and bondage and a host of terrors.

It is better to fall into added disrepute with an enemy than to alienate a would-be-friend.

There once was a golden age, because golden hearts beat in it. If it come again, it will scarcely be through scientific progress.

When genius seems to work disregarding rule, we may be sure it has assimilated to itself whatever is best in every rule.


## II   The White Sail

*The White Sail and Other Poems,* which appeared in 1887 under the imprint of Ticknor and Company, attested to Louise's admission to the circle of Ticknor and Fields. In one sense, its contents hardly moved out of dry dock at number 148 Charles Street where the Fields' presided over arrivals and sailings of literary cargo for America's best consumers. (Annie Fields liked Louise, who was known in the aviary of her songsters as "the Linnet," as Celia Thaxter, another favorite visitor, was classified as "the Sandpiper.")[14] But *The White Sail* was inflated with artificial respiration. If *Goose-Quill Papers* had diffused the must of archives, rather than the freshness of a girl's breath, *The White Sail* foundered in the shallows of the literary clique to which lionizing had introduced her. Self-conscious but talented *artistes* like Alice Brown and Louise Chandler Moulton entertained Louise on the back slopes of Beacon Hill and at Rutland Square. They lived near the Common, but they did not belong to the community; and, if Boston's Cabots "spoke only to God," they spoke only to each other. Their *camaraderie* was closer still because of the growing alienation of the artist in America's *Philistia.* Louise nearly became another house plant in their esthetic hothouse.

Of course, there were creditable poems in *The White Sail* that the

tangled forests of bohemia could not chill to violet-size—the delicate
opening couplet of "Paula's Epitaph," for example, Grecianly
elegiac in its simplicity and evocative of the finality of death. "Pass
you by with gentle tread,/ This was Paula, who is dead." "The
Wild Ride," yet to be perfected for inclusion in *Happy Ending,*
is already powerful in its pounding anapestic hexameters and
in its surrealist painting of the terrors of a bad dream:

> I hear in my heart, I hear in its ominous pulses
> All day, on the road, the hoofs of invisible horses,
> All night, from their stalls, the importunate pawing and neighing.

If the title poem, "The White Sail," suffers by patching Romantic
form and interpretation on the classical Greek legend of Theseus'
return from the Minotaur, the poem "Tarpeia" is integrally Roman
in the severity of its justice and in the soldier-sonority of its marching
cadence. Its authenticity, moreover, derives added strength from
Guiney's fiercely held convictions that loyalty is the first virtue and that
treachery is the basest sin. Because, for unexplained reasons, she
chose not to preserve her story of Tarpeia, "the Traitor of Rome," in
either *A Roadside Harp* (1893) or in *Happy Ending* (1909), some
selections may be useful to convey its power.[15] No attenuating
sophistication has  sapped the strength of the lines, and perhaps
Louise was questioning in "Tarpeia" the possibility of her own
seduction by the glittering blandishments of mannerism:

> Woe: Lightly to part with one's soul as the sea
>     with its foam!
> Woe to Tarpeia, Tarpeia, daughter of Rome!
> It was night in the camp, with the moon looking
>     chill as she went:
> It was morn when the innocent stranger strayed
>     into the tent.
>
> The hostile Sabini were pleased as one meshing a bird,
> She sang for them there in the forest: they smiled
>     as they heard.
>
>           .   .   .   .   .   .   .   .   .   .   .   .   .
>
> The chief sat apart, brow in hand, and with
>     elbow on knee:
> The armlets he wore were aglow, and a wonder to see:

Exquisite artifice, whorls of barbaric design,
Frost's fixed mimicry; orbic imaginings fine,

.   .   .   .   .   .   .   .   .   .   .   .   .   .   .   .   .

And the glory thereof sent fever and fire to her eye
"I had never such trinkets!" she sighed. (Like a lute
      was her sigh.)

"Were they mine at the word, and mine for the token
      all told,
Now the citadel sleeps, now my father the keeper
      is old.
If I go by the way that I know, and thou followest hard,
If yet at the touch of Tarpeia the gates be unbarred?"

The Chief trembled sharply for joy, then drew rein
      on his soul:
"Of all this arm beareth I swear I will yield thee
      the whole."

.   .   .   .   .   .   .   .   .   .   .   .   .   .   .   .   .

Her nostril upraised, as a fawn's on the arrowy air,
She sped. In a serpentine gleam up the precipice stair
They climbed in her traces, they closed on their evil
      swift star:
She bent to the latches, and swung the great portal
      ajar.

Forgot as they passed, and half-tearful for wounded belief,
"The bracelets!" she pleaded. Then faced her the lion-like
      Chief,

.   .   .   .   .   .   .   .   .   .   .   .   .   .   .   .   .

"This left arm shall nothing begrudge thee. Accept. Find
      it sweet,
Give, too, O my brothers!" The jewels he flung
      at her feet,

The jewels hard-heavy; she stooped to them, flushing
      with dread;
But the shield he flung after: it clanged on her
      beautiful head:

         .   .   .   .   .   .   .   .   .   .   .   .   .   .

> And with "Hail benefactress!" upon her they hurled
>     in their zeal
> Death: agate and iron; death: chyroprase, beryl
>     and steel;
> A mountain of shields! And through the least crevice
>     behold
> In a torrent-like gush pouring out the inordinate
>     gold!
>
> Pyramidal gold! The sumptuous monument won
> By the deed they had loved her for, doing—and loathed
>     her for, done.
>
> Woe: lightly to part with one's soul as the sea with its foam!
> Woe to Tarpeia, Tarpeia, traitor to Rome.

When Horace Scudder reviewed *The White Sail and Other Poems* in *Atlantic* several months after its publication,[16] he began his review by politely acknowledging that "the expectation with which we greeted Miss Guiney's *Songs at the Start* . . . has been much more than realized in her latest book." Although he admitted that "Tarpeia" and "The Wild Ride" certainly represented an advance, he went to work with the editor's incisive scalpel, cutting into the morbid growths that jeopardized her future health—ones fostered, in part, by the unsalubrious climate of air-tight salons of the Back Bay. To Scudder, Louise was "so oblique and allusive" that she shot wide of her mark. She was "so ambitious to be terse and sinewy" that she tied "knots into her sentences," lumping her lines into masses that achieved less strength than a "clumsy affectation of virility." Her poems needed less connoisseurship "in words" and "more growing life"; otherwise, she was heading for the sterility of "a linguistic museum." He was right, for the net of language had become more important than the quarry, life. The cryptic style was becoming a crypt.

# Mouth of the Lion

H APPILY for Louise, she had other preoccupations at this time which enabled her to evade the butterfly net of bohemia. To be sure, she continued in the circles which made the 1880's and early 1890's her blithest years; for, if anything, she multiplied her associations and activities in the exciting fraternity of the art world by encouraging Fred Holland Day and Herbert Copeland to rival England's Kelmscott Press with home-grown American art editions;[1] by joining Ralph Adams Cram and Bernard Berenson in their William Morris-inspired medievalism; by editing *The Knight Errant* and projecting the abortive "Twentieth Century";[2] and by frequenting the Boston Athenaeuum where Charles Knowles Bolton, the librarian, also took part in the pseudo-monastic charade of Cram's "Order of the White Rose."[3] Even in the midst of such arty circles, however, Louise retained her freshness and honesty. Looking back at those Pre-Raphaelite posturings, their projects dissipated and their productions few, Cram recalled Louise as "the most vital and creative personal influence in the lives of all of us who gathered together at this time."[4] Looking back at him, no less affectionately, she called him "a lunatic angel."[5]

The fortunate preoccupation which carried her, periodically, out of the whirl and back to reality was dictated by her "obligation to pay tithes"; for her father's estate was dwindling. She had to find work, and the invitation of President Seelye of newly established Smith College to make application seemed not only God-sent but congenial: "Your name has been suggested for a position as teacher of English literature." Although Louise responded with alacrity, she was informed, rather curtly, by the signing secretary that "you have not gone extensively enough into the study of English literature to meet our present demands."[6] No complaint at this rebuff can be found in her letters or elsewhere; she merely redoubled her efforts to compile in book form the numerous articles which, since 1884, she had been contributing for support to the popular children's magazine, *Wide Awake*. If humble, it was not humbling;

for Louise was naturally close to a child's purity and fantasy. More-over, such writing brought her out of the stifling salons and back to childhood's world of wonder in which poetry has its source.


## I  Brownies and Bogles

*Wide Awake* in itself was not hack work from Grub Street, but it was one of some seventy-five English-language publications that catered to the boom in juveniles in America between 1885 and 1905 before the cinema and television claimed this audience.[7] Of these, it ranked with the most popular, *Youth's Companion, Golden Argosy, American Boy;* and it rivaled Scribner's durable "Illustrated Magazine for Boys and Girls," the still famous *St. Nicholas,* with which it merged in 1893.[8] Daniel Lothrop had founded *Wide Awake* in 1875; and Margaret Sidney, author of *Five Little Peppers and How They Grew,* was on the staff. Sarah Orne Jewett and Louise Chandler Moulton were regular contributors, and Edmund H. Garrett frequently illustrated its monthly quarto editions.

In 1886, Palmer Cox, editor of *St. Nicholas,* had launched the "brownie" vogue that was to run its course into the early 1920's.[9] To capitalize on this rage, Lothrop and Company entered the field in 1888 with *Brownies and Bogles,* a compilation of twelve stories by Louise, previously featured in *Wide Awake* under the title "Fairy Folk All." Louise, who had revealed her natural oneness with children in the delightful letters to Margaret Haskell of Auburndale (*Letters,* I, 14–21, 69–71)[10] and her empathy with childhood in her analysis of Vaughan and her articles on "Digby Dolben" and "Childhood in English Seventeenth Century Poetry,"[11] brought exceptional credentials to *Brownies and Bogles.*

In a late letter to the Reverend Geoffrey Bliss, S.J., Louise's research collaborator on *Recusant Poets,* she tagged these qualifica-tions unintentionally: "My hugged-most bit of Phariseeism is the sense that I never taught nobody nuffin'!"[12] Indeed, no magisterial superiority obtrudes between her and the young reader; she simply shares experience and never imposes it upon the defenseless-defensive child. She paid children the ultimate respect of treating their fantasy world with their own high seriousness—without talking down to them and without watering down the considerable scholarship demanded by her census of Mab's realm and its tributary states: neckin, kobolds,

elves, leprechauns, dwarfs, goblins, sprites, trolls, and banshees. She read over two hundred volumes to record their origins and to distinguish their habits from Norway to Persia. Better, she enjoyed it all. Otherwise, one could not account for her awareness of how big "the little people" really are. Her introduction is as sane as it is sweet:

A fairy is a humorous person sadly out of fashion at present, who has had, nevertheless, in the actor's phrase, a long and prosperous run on this planet. When we speak of fairies nowadays, we think only of small sprites who live in a kingdom of their own, with manners, laws, and privileges very different from ours. But there was a time when "fairy" suggested also the knights and ladies of romance, about whom fine spirited tales were told when the world was younger. Spenser's Faery Queen, for instance, deals with dream people, beautiful and brave, as do the old stories of Arthur and Roland; people who either never lived, or who, having lived, were glorified and magnified out of all kinship with common men. Our fairies are fairies in the modern sense. We will make it a rule, from the beginning, that they must be small, and we will put out any who are above the regulation height .... By and by you may care to study them for themselves; at present, we shall be very high-handed with the science of folk-lore, and pay no attention whatever to learned gentlemen, who quarrel so foolishly about these things that it is not helpful, nor even funny, to listen to them.[13]

The last chapter of *Brownies and Bogles* ("The Passing of the Little People") is equally artful in its transition from the child's "willing suspension of disbelief" back to a world of realism where, if adjustments must be made, dreams, somehow, must also be kept. Guiney shows true art in effecting the passage:

Goodbye, then, to the army of vanishing "gentry," and to their steadfast friends, and to you, children dear! who are the guardians of their wild unwritten records .... Keep the fairies in kindly memory. They and their history have an enchanting value, which need never be outgrown nor set aside; and to the gravest mind they bring much which is beautiful, humane and suggestive.

We have found that believers in the Little People were not so wrong, after all; and that the eye claiming to have seen a fairy saw, verily, a sight quite as astonishing. Let us think as gently of other myths to which men have given zeal, awe and admiration, of every faith hereafter which seems to us odd and mistaken. For many things which are not true in the exact sense, are yet dear to Truth; and follow her as a baby's tripping tongue lisps the language of its mother, not very successfully, but still with loyalty, and with a meaning which attentive ears can always catch.[14]

Years later, Louise called *Brownies and Bogles* "that useless
youngster book of mine . . . wholly out of print since about 1890."[15]
But she had built better than she knew, for the commonsense sym-
pathetically made palatable to children during a "brownie" vogue
had blossomed into a perennial wisdom for her juvenile readers and
herself. Thereby, she had evaded the stranglehold of her bookish
friends; she had disciplined her native endowment for speaking the
truth ("Out of the mouths of babes"); and she had preserved her
Vaughan-like wonder before the poetry and the mystery of life. Such
recognition underlay her advice in 1896 to Van Allen about "primitive" versus "modern" Christianity: "How can countless generations
keep a dogma . . . without accidental (not essential) accretions? Is
not the accretion a proof of love and long meditations? . . . If
Shakespeare had had no commentaries, wouldn't it look as if the race
cared not a pin for Shakespeare?"[16] That view of basic mythic
truth illuminated her explanation of superstition to Gwenllian
Morgan, in 1902:" "Superstition, after all, is too much faith, an ex-
crescence on true faith . . . . The Reformers . . . brought it forward
as . . . a catchword when they were set on destroying the Poetry and
Romance of Catholicism . . . . They wanted everything prosy and
practical, so they called the immemorial loveliness of ritual 'fuss' and
flung it away."[17]

## II    *Animals and Nature*

Children's next of kin, animals and nature, also kept Louise-the-
lionized from being prematurely devoured. Her fondness for (indeed,
identity with) St. Bernards has won her the not unacceptable title
of Laureate to Dog-dom. Among such poems are "Davy" and "To
the Memory of a Dog" and, among her essays, "Reminiscences of a
Fine Gentleman," "Brother," and "The Puppy." Her sympathy for
pets fills her correspondence, tangentially darts in and out of comments on books or religion, and also culminates in almost jesuitical
casuistry to validate their immortality.[18] But the empathy was not
canine-confined; it was extended to all animals. At the zoo, she
immortalized the lions in the *Patrins* classic, "The Captives": "If the
Oriental religious have any mission to discharge in our behalf, let
them teach us speedily, through any gracious superstition whatever,
their grave respect for animal life. . . . The captives have borne their
fate, yet not quite dispassionately. They lose, behind bars, day by

day, something of themselves hard to part with. . . . What if there should be freedom again for them, beyond death? Some thought as profound surges this morning in a vast antiphonal cry among the tanks and cages, and shakes, in passing, the soul of man."[19]

Nature also, for Louise, was a salutary antidote against infection by the miasma of bohemia's underground and by musty libraries. Nature was not just sanely restorative, as in the case of Wordsworth; it was a creative kinship almost pagan-primitive, as with Emily Brontë.[20] Rural Auburndale afforded her a happy retreat from the city, as did the delight of her romps along the Charles River or through the Belmont hills. So did the Wayland woods and the beaches and marshes of Scituate when she visited her friend Thomas Parsons, the first American to translate the *Divine Comedy*.[21] The sense of healing restoration vibrates in the long-disputed "Out in the Fields with God",[22] often erroneously attributed to Elizabeth Barrett Browning:

> The little cares that fretted me,
> I lost them yesterday
> Among the fields above the sea,
> Among the winds at play.

The more characteristic Brontë note, which could be overheard in Louise's "Gloucester Harbor," the opening lyric of *Songs at the Start,* is louder in insistence on the ominous and the stormy in two poems collected in *Happy Ending,* "The Squall" and "Romans in Dorset".

### The Squall

> While all was glad
> It seemed our birch-tree had,
> That August hour, intelligence of death;
> For warningly against the eaves she beat
> Her body old, lamenting, prophesying,
> And the hot breath
> Of ferny hollows nestled at her feet
> Spread out in startled sighing.[23]

### Romans in Dorset

> A stupor on the heath,
> And wrath along the sky;

> Space everywhere: beneath
> A flat and treeless world for us, and darkest noon on high.

> Sullen quiet below,
> But storm in upper air!
> A wind from long ago,
> In mouldy chambers of the cloud had ripped an arras there, . . .[24]

Guiney's sympathy with the mythic-mysterious had convinced Alice Brown that, however "Christian in belief," Louise was "pagan in her listening nerves"; she was in tune, in fact, with an order antecedent to civilization.[25] Bliss Carman, another writer friend, reacted similarly to Louise's "Alexandriana": "paganism." Though Louise protested this analysis to her confidant W. H. Van Allen[26] and suggested that "natural religion" might have been more correct, some confirmation of the Brown-Carman opinion accumulates from other Guiney poems, notably the octave of the sonnet "In a Ruin, after a Thunderstorm." Caught high on the broken battlements of Rochester Castle during a sudden cloudburst, her first reaction to the elemental tumult had been instinctive defiance:

> Keeper of the Norman, old to flood and cloud!
> Thou dost reproach me with thy sunset look,
> That in our common menace I forsook
> Hope, the last fear, and stood impartial proud:
> Almost, almost, while ether spake aloud,
> Death from the smoking stones my spirit shook
> Into thy hollow as leaves into a brook,
> No more than they by heaven's assassin cowed.[27]

In the concluding sestet, she did attempt, repentantly, to retrieve a Christian humility. However theologically orthodox, it is, poetically, an afterthought: "Breathe on me better valor." The same deep roots in nature disclose themselves in another sonnet, "Heathenesse," in which Louise frankly acknowledges nature as "sister great and dear"—notwithstanding her "Catholic's Ready Answer" rebuke to Wordsworth for longing to "see Proteus rising from the sea."[28] The "Two Irish Peasant Songs," first included in *A Roadside Harp* and reprinted in *Happy Ending,*[29] not only possess a primitive soil-strength but also a frankly erotic response to the surge of love in the springtime: "Why from me that's

young should the wild tears fall?/ . . . The foolishness is on me, and
the wild tears fall!"

Children, animals, and nature, each in its way, rescued Miss Guiney
from complete wreckage on the siren coasts of bohemia. The voyage
to England, in the company of her mother aboard the *Pavonia,* in
May, 1889, removed her from the rock-bound shores of New England altogether. If, after Elmhurst, Auburndale's leisurely studies
had been her Miltonian "Horton" period, this trip was her consummating grand tour—as well as the expenditure of the last of her dead
father's legacy.

CHAPTER 5

# Abroad

## I  *English Interval: 1889–1891*

ENGLAND was for Louise an old home far more than for Hawthorne during his service in the Liverpool consulate. London,
where she established residence with her Mother, cast a spell never to
be broken. Its palpable history deepened her conviction that she had
"always been organically European,"[1] and it also evoked poetic
response to the Chapel of Edward the Confessor in Westminster
Abbey; to the Reading Room of the British Museum; to the spires
of Oxford.

When she first entered "the cool enshadowed port of poets," in
Westminster Abbey, it made her feel "a little sail long due." Rapt
in its dim aisles, she broke "tryst with transitory things 'to' seal . . .
a marriage and a peace eternal."[2] The nine sonnets written later
at Oxford (and privately printed as a Christmas gift for friends in
1895) repeat the same communion: "At home in quarries of old
Christendom."[3] The sonnet, "In the Reading Room of the British
Museum," renewed her dedication to letters like vows at an altar of
self-renouncing scholarship:

> Praise be the moon of books! that doth above
> A world of men, the sunken Past behold,
>
> .  .  .  .  .  .  .  .  .  .  .
>
> Nothing are days and deeds to such as they,
> While in this liberal house thy face is bright.[4]

Bookmen, too, received her homage and laid the foundation of
enduring friendships: Dr. Alexander Grosart, the antiquarian-
collector; Dr. Richard Garnett, Keeper of the Books in the British
Museum; and Bertram Dobell, London bookseller and editor of
seventeenth-century poets. Herbert E. Clarke, with whom Louise
had already opened the correspondence which was to last until his
death in 1912, met her for the first time and introduced her to literary

London as an old friend and as a promising talent.[5] In Ireland to read her paper on Sir Walter Raleigh in the spring of 1890, she began the acquaintance with the Sigersons and with Clement Shorter which would fructify later in her edition of Clarence Mangan and in her biography of Robert Emmet.[6] In Wales, she made her first sortie into Vaughan country, to be explored subsequently in the company of Alice Brown. But London was capital of her heart. In quick retrospect after returning to the United States, she could write to host Clarke: "What wouldn't I give to be on Fleet St., again, with a fog on my spectacles and the liberal clink of ha'pennies in my pocket! . . . bless all bookstalls, hurdie-gurdies, bobbies, out-of-door games, chimes . . . and snails on sale, in my name."[7]

The year 1890 was, indeed, a bright and busy one in London: Browning's funeral had just been held at Westminster Abbey on the last day of the old year; Victoria's Diamond Jubilee Celebration and the opening of the Tudor Exhibition dominated the new. Louise attended them all as a precariously paid correspondent for the Boston *Post,*[8] but her reports were not always complimentary. For example, Queen Victoria, the Hanoverian, could hardly seduce Louise from her Jacobite's fealty to liege-lord Stuarts. Victoria was that "money-saving, gillie-adoring, etiquette-blinded, pudgy, plodding, unspiritual, unliterary, mercantile, dowdy, sparkless, befogged, continuous Teuton lady,"[9] whose prime minister, rectitudinous Gladstone, was "a born archdeacon."[10] "How could Van Dyke have posed her?" Louise asked. The Tudor Exhibition of portraits at the New Gallery also depressed her by the dullness of its subjects. Plainly, master Holbein lacked the elegant material that surrounded Charles I in Van Dyke's studio. "Elizabeth-Schmiddy" *Hausfrauen,* the Tudor dames had neither the aroma of manners nor the mystery of sex: "No kirtled aristocracy of any age or country was ever so flat and dozy."[11]

## II  *Social Justice*

Nor did Louise miss the underside of London town. Like provincial Hawthorne, freshly arrived from pastoral New England, she was appalled by the sprawling slums now thoroughly begrimed by William Blake's dark satanic mills: "Heaven thickens over, Heaven that cannot cure/Her tear by day, her fevered smile by night."[12]

She saw strikers marching in Hyde Park, like ghosts of buried
Chartists:

> Hither, upon the Georgian idlers' tread,
> Up spacious ways the lindens interleave,
> Clouding the royal air since yester-eve,
> Come men bereft of time and scant of bread,
> Loud, who were dumb, immortal, who were dead,
> Through the cowed world their kingdom to retrieve.[13]

She asked: "What ails thee, England? Altar, mart, and grange/
Dream of the knife by night." Even the townhouses of the rich
in Belgravia looked coldly down on the wretches huddling for shelter
beneath their porticoes:

> When, after dawn, the lordly houses hide
> Till you fall foul of it, some piteous guest
> (Some girl the damp stones gather to their breast,
> Her gold hair rough, her rebel garment wide,
> Who sleeps, with all that luck and life denied
> Camped round, and dreams how seaward and southwest,
> Blue over Devon farms the smoke-rings rest
> And sheep and lambs ascend the lit hillside) . . . .[14]

While standing at the grave of William Hazlitt, Louise had a vision
of a revolutionary justice that would overcome: "Therefore sleep
safe, thou dear and battling spirit . . . /Sleep safe in dark Soho: the
stars are shining/ . . . the People marches."[15] She found greater
reassurance of a new dawn in the unquenchable spirit of the poor
themselves, however degraded; for the hurdy-gurdy of their organ
grinder had its own inspiring call to arms:

In a City Street

> Though sea and mount have beauty and this but what it can,
> Thrice fairer than their life and life here battling in
>      the van,
> The tragic gleam, the mist and grime,
> The dread endearing stain of time,
> The sullied heart of man.
>
>        .   .   .   .   .   .   .   .   .   .   .   .   .   .
>
> The bells, the dripping gable, the tavern's corner glare;
> The cab in firefly darting; the barrel-organ air,
> While one by one, or two by two

> The hatless babes are waltzing through
> The gutters of the Square.[16]

If her hope faltered, there was always America, beyond the western horizon, still open to courage and teeming with opportunity. The sight of the Stars and Stripes flapping in the breeze from the mast of a merchantman tied up in the Thames River was a clarion of liberty for all:

### In the Docks

> Where the bales thunder till the day is done,
> And the wild sounds with wilder odours cope;
> Where over crouching sail and coiling rope,
> Lascar and Moor along the gangway run;
> Where stifled Thames spreads in the pallid sun,
> A hive of anarchy from slope to slope;
> Flag of my birth, my liberty, my hope,
> I see thee at the masthead, joyous one!
> O thou good guest! So oft as, young and warm,
> To the home-wind thy hoisted colours bound,
> Away, away from this too thoughtful ground,
> Sodden with human trespass and despair,
> Thee only, from the desert, from the storm,
> A sick mind follows into Eden air.[17]

### III   *Visitor from America*

More than nostalgia for America reclaimed Louise. By mid-summer of 1889, Fred Holland Day of Boston and Norwood had followed the Guiney trail to London. His ostensible purpose was expansion of his Keats collection; but this newest interest, among his many hobbies, was indissociable from Louise Guiney. They were distant relatives[18] and intimate companions, especially in their early devotion to Keats, who later became a cult before the turn of the century. More accurately, they were its leaders until Louis Arthur Holman[19] and Amy Lowell[20] appeared later on the scene; for Louise and Day had been dynamic precursors in the recovery of Keats's reputation and in the stimulation of Keats scholarship.[21] Together they were active agents in establishing the Keats Memorial at Hampstead. Day spent part of his considerable

fortune in the purchase of Fanny Brawne's letters to Fanny Keats; and the more energetic Louise led him, literally, to his rare find of the Brawne-Keats letters in Madrid. She wrote and lectured on "Johnny";[22] he collected memorabilia and dreamed of his unwritten book on Keats and Fanny Brawne for the next fifty years until his death in 1933.

When Day's jealously guarded hoard was finally consigned to Lionel McColvin, chief librarian of the Keats Memorial at Hampstead,[23] he had acknowledged his debt to Louise by stipulating that the letters were not to be exhibited until 1961, the hundredth anniversary of her birth; but Day had never shown the originals to her during her lifetime. Significantly, when the memorial was dedicated in 1893 with the unveiling of Anne Whitney's bust of Keats in the Hampstead Parish Church, the press mentioned Guiney among the donors, but not Day—although Day attended the ceremony in company with such other illustrious sponsors as sculptress Whitney, James Russell Lowell, Professor Charles Eliot Norton, Mrs. James T. Fields, and Thomas Bailey Aldrich.[24]

Day was always on the fringe as publisher of deluxe editions, briefly, to the 1890's; as amateur art-photographer (hundreds of pictures and transparencies of Louise are among the papers which he deposited in the Library of Congress); and as collector of Keatsiana and Guiney letters. Hopefully he believed that posterity would recognize him by including him in any new edition of Louise's sparkling correspondence: "There should be a volume of correspondence issued. I have never known in the whole line of English Epistolary Literature an example to match her in brilliance and nimbleness of felicitous expression."[25] However, only her letters to him remain, almost a thousand, deposited after his death by his attorney, Julius H. Tuttle, in the Library of Congress in 1934; for his letters to her were probably among those burned by Alice Brown after Louise's death.

## IV   *Keats Trail*

Day's voyage to England, a few months in the wake of the Guineys, was not altogether a surprise; for he had been calling with increasing frequency on Miss Guiney since 1884. His gifts, in number and value, had also multiplied. When Louise launched the shallow-draft

*White Sail* with a dedication to their "Johnny" ("Keats, I lay here against thy moon-lit, storm-shaken pillar, my garland of a day"), Day reacted, on Christmas, 1888, with a present guaranteed to thrill her: a copy of Haydon's life-mask of their mutual idol. Later he sent her a precious lock of Keats's hair, which she kept in a crystal-set ring until she donated the treasure to her beloved Bodleian Library, which also received from her an equally precious encased lock of Robert Louis Stevenson's hair and her rare first edition of Vaughan's *Thalia Rediviva.*

Day's pursuit of the Guineys had probably been expedited by Louise's letter to him of May 28, 1889, informing him that, incredible as it sounded, Fanny Keats y de Llanos was alive in Madrid.[26] Her "Let's go to Madrid on a tricycle!" may have cooled his ardor; for, after reaching London, he preferred scouring Hampstead and its environs for Keats relics while enjoying Louise's company and explaining the tandem arrangement to a still Daisy-Millerish society by their absolving "Carter Cousin" relationship. He did exert himself sufficiently to acquire Señora de Llanos address from Harry Buxton Forman. But, when he shook himself free of Hampstead and London bookstalls and crossed the Channel to Paris, he abruptly turned north for a holiday in Brussels! There, after direct inquiry to Madrid, he contacted Señora de Llanos by post; and she promptly replied, in three consecutive exchanges. Whereupon, with characteristic unpredictability, notwithstanding Louise's pleading letters to follow up his strike, he sailed for Boston in November. On December 16, Fanny Keats y de Llanos died at the age of eighty-six.

When Day returned to London the following June (1890), Louise was at the boat-train to greet him. Excited and pert, with her hair in a pigtail, she was "comfortably innocent and shabby, with not a care in the world."[27] Warm welcome notwithstanding, Day was cool to the prospect of a trip to Spain for a conference with the de Llanos heirs. He loitered about London into November. To insure completion of his mission, the Guineys, mother and daughter, accompanied him to Paris and put him bodily aboard the Madrid Express. By the time they had returned to London, discouraged from sightseeing in Paris and Amiens by the approaching winter, Day, by virtue of his conquest of the hospitable de Llanos, had his prize in hand; thirty-one letters written by Fanny Brawne Lindon to Fanny Keats y de Llanos, between 1820 and 1824.

En route to America with his find, Day stopped in London to present Louise with a lock of "Johnny's" curls. But, as already noted, he did not let Louise see, much less handle, the valuable letters—then, or ever. Rebuffed in one attempt to get permission to publish from Herbert V. Lindon, Fanny Brawne's son and heir, Day carried the letters back to Norwood, Massachusetts, where he hoarded them for forty-three sterile years. Otherwise, Day continued to be generous to Louise, if somewhat more distant as he became more pronouncedly eccentric; and he remained her confidant in hours of need. He published five of her books handsomely, almost as if he had remained in the business principally on her account. He turned his Beacon Hill apartment over to mother and daughter when straitened circumstances required their residence in Boston and forced them to list the Auburndale property for sale. He bought Louise's little seaside cottage ("Shanty Guiney") at Five Islands, Maine; and he promptly rechristened it "Castle Guiney" when she cut her ties with America after her mother's death. When he died, his will stipulated that his ashes be strewn from an airplane over this spot where they had spent happy vacations together.

Was Day impotent? Had he been emasculated by the apron strings of twin Victorian matriarchs—"Lady Day," as Louise regularly referred to his mother, and "Aunt Jenny," as he called hers? There is little doubt of his love for Louise; and to anyone reading her letters to him, there is no doubt that she was a born lover, eager for his company. Certainly, they never ceased to be friends, in shared confidence and concern. Was he, essentially, a collector whose *pièce de résistance* was Louise? Patently, hers was no spirit for pinning to a butterfly board or for confining to a curio cabinet. But, undoubtedly, Day was among the influences diverting her from creativity to collecting.

# Back in Boston

L OUISE'S "grand tour" ended early in 1891. Well before spring she and her mother were back in Auburndale. Financial worry has always overshadowed them during the *wanderjahr,* although Louise had put a good face on it in her letters to Fred Holland Day. ("I am as usual, out of pocket. My debts from Ameriky now amount to $760.00. How's that?"[1]) But she had been touring under no illusion. Her overseas reports mailed back to the Boston *Post* had been a contractual arrangement to assure some support. Her articles published in American magazines during this period testify to her concern, as well as to her industry: "Reminiscences of a Fine Gentleman," *Catholic World* (August, 1889); "English Lyrics Under the First Charles," *Harper's New Monthly* (May, 1890); "Sir Walter Raleigh of Youghal in the County of Cork," *Atlantic Monthly* (December, 1890).

The same industry had accumulated copious other literary materials for reworking at home. The first to materialize was *A Summer in England,*[2] a handbook for American lady tourists, which Louise prepared in collaboration with Alice Brown, who had been co-editor with her of the *Pilgrim Scrip,* "a little club paper" published by the Women's Rest Tour Association. An outgrowth of the periodical, the handbook was the first of a series of five editions, the last of which is dated March 5, 1900. Louise's knowledge of London and the English countryside and her experience in living economically made her a reliable guide.

### I  *Footlights and Fancy*

Throughout 1892 a decidedly French trail winds through her writings, from her addiction to Gallicisms in her letters,[3] to her adaptation of French plays for the stage, to her biography of *Monsieur Henri.* The biography had been sketched in two consecutive installments in the *Catholic World* (May and June, 1888) a year before her first crossing to England and the Continent.[4] Although

there is no evidence in extant letters incontrovertibly affirming her visit to Brittany during 1889–91, it seems likely that she did travel in the *Vendée* within this period. The published letters suffer a gap here—only one letter included: to her Auburndale neighbor, Mrs. Haskell, dated August 3, 1889. But the internal evidence of *Monsieur Henri* strongly suggests an on-the-scene familiarity with the terrain described, as does her correspondence with the Count de Chabot now in the Guiney Collection at Holy Cross College. So does her personal inscription of acknowledgments penned, for revision, into her own copy of the little book: "to the *Curé* and *le Vicaire* of St. Aubin-de-Baubigné, who ... brightened my frosty travels in the *Bocage*."⁵

Her dabbling in French drama was flirtation or potboiler, or both. Her adaptation of Alexandre Dumas' *Le Demi-Monde* was staged in Boston and New York in 1892 as *The Crust of Society*. When William Seymour and John Stetson produced it at the Globe Theatre in Boston, it apparently met some success; for Louise wrote to her old friend Ada Langley, the popular actress (then married to Frederick Briggs): "J. Stetson, Esq., ... wants me to do Émile Augier's 'Le Mariage d'Olymphe.' OH CRACKY! It is huge fun to make a living out of other folk's brains, ... "⁶ Charles E. L. Wingate confirmed the rumor in the *Critic's* "Boston Letter" of September 2, 1893: "I can also give the news to Boston that Manager Stetson of the *Globe Theatre* will have another new play from Miss Guiney's pen for next year. She has translated Emil [sic] Augier's 'Mariage d'Olymphe'—a work never seen before on the American stage."⁷

In the same man-about-town style, after lauding the success in the previous year of *The Demi-Monde,* Wingate announced that Miss Guiney currently had a sequel, *The Prince's Tragedy,* in rehearsal at the Grand Opera House, in preparation for a Thanksgiving opening: the first English adaptation of Casimir Delavigne's *Les Enfants d'Édouard.* Wingate even named the cast: Olive Homans, of *Little Lord Fauntleroy* fame, to star,⁸ supported by Joseph Haworth in the male lead and Kitty Dooling (Louise's Elmhurst classmate), besides a number of Harvard boys and friends of the young author "among the supernumeraries." Both productions aborted. But years later, desperate to sell any work, Louise was still trying to market "The Prince's Tragedy" among English producers.⁹

## II  *The Knight Errant*

Yet authentic drama pervades *Monsieur Henri,* published by Harper's in 1892. Indeed, her biography of the youthful Count de La Rochejaquelin borders on melodrama. "Monsieur Henri," soldier, loyalist, and loser, was bound to compel her admiration. He stood beside Marie Antoinette until the last moment on the night of August 10, 1792 when the Paris mobs stormed the Tuileries. He escaped across France and raised an army of volunteers "For God and Country." Against overwhelming odds, he won victory after victory, initially, over the "Blues" dispatched by the Committee of Public Safety against the diehard *Vendée.* He was chivalrous in victory, indomitable in reversal; and he died advancing alone, hardly having attained his majority: "a type of young French manhood ere it had grown wholly modern and complex, ... a straggler from the pageant of the ancestral Crusades ... a hard hitter, and a dear fellow."[10]

Louise was not unaware of the advent of the modern antihero or of Henri's own shortcomings. She modestly subtitled his biography "A Footnote to History"; and she candidly answered her own questionings: "Virtually, what did he amount to? What loud testimony of him is left? To the man of facts ... the best answers are, Nothing and None."[11] But, though she admitted that Henri was "a boy so pyrotechnically French that we smile over him," she agreed with George Eliot that the "greatest gift the hero leaves his race is to have been a hero":

His chivalry went to the upholding of kings; all he did has a sole value of loyalty, and we may dispute the application of it .... He stands among the serious, war-worn leaders of the insurrection like a fairy prince, with a bright, absurd glamour. He was all that children look for in a tale, and he had no moral .... Because of his shortcomings, rather than in spite of them, his arm seems laden with everlasting sheaves. May there not be, in the economy of nature, a waste which is thrift, a daring which is prudence, a folly which is wisdom ineffable?[12]

She must have had Henri in mind when she set the same high goal for herself in "The Kings." For she, too, dared challenge the times rather than grovel in a marketplace that left no pedestal for heroes:

> While Kings of eternal evil
> Yet darken the hills about,

> Thy part is with broken sabre
> To rise on the last redoubt;
>
> To fear not sensible failure,
> Nor covet the game at all,
> But fighting, fighting, fighting,
> Die, driven against the wall,![13]

In telling Henri's story, Guiney was not just repaying an old debt to the *émigrée* nuns who had taught her at Elmhurst. Nor was she only defending the Old Faith enshrined in her heart by their legends of an *ancien régime*. She was recounting, with gripping vividness, the history of a people's rebellion against tyranny: "a spontaneous rising of the free peasants against what they believed to be the spirit of rapine and injustice."[14] Carlyle's *French Revolution* had dismissed the Vendean War as an episode, "blown into flame and fury by theological and seigneurial bellows."[15] For Louise, it was another Concord and Lexington, with simple Minute Men defending their rights against foreign hirelings. To her, the real heroes were the people and their peasant generals, Jacques Cathelineau and Jean-Nicholas Stofflet. Glamorous Henri, with his hit-and-run raids out of the *bocage,* was a French Francis Marion.

The style of *Monsieur Henri* shows clearly that the general's daughter is back in his saddle again. Her prose is vigorous, even virile. The narrative moves rapidly, marred only where it essays dialogue; for then the few speeches verge on the heroic-dramatic, explicable partly by the nature of traditional French oratory. But she described troop movements with a soldier's grasp. She seemed to know every foot of the *bocage* and the disposition of the towns on its perimeter. Her account of the desperate, futile thrust into Brittany to open a seaport is first-rate military reporting. Her detail of the aftermath, as the beaten provincials attempt to recross the Loire River in winter, has the impact of tragedy. Plainly, the cause is lost, although Henri has more engagements to win before his death at Trémentines-sur-Nouaillé.

Always a severe critic of her own books, Louise was partial to this one. She had fifty signed copies bound in the Chollen plaid which had been Henri's distinctive badge. She fairly covered her personal copy with notes for revision, hoping vainly into her last years for a

second edition. Heroes were too precious to let die; and Henri du
Verger was her "Knight Errant." Although Donatello's statue of
Saint George had inspired the poem, the sculptor's St. George
was knight-generic for Louise's knight-in-carnate:

> Sprits of old that bore me,
> And set me meek of mind,
> Between great dreams before me,
> And deeds as great behind,
> Knowing humanity my star
> As first abroad I ride,
> Shall help me wear with every scar
> Honour at eventide.
>
> Let claws of lightning clutch me
> From summer's groaning cloud,
> Or ever malice touch me,
> And glory make me proud.
> Oh, give my youth, my faith, my sword,
> Choice of the heart's desire:
> A short life in the saddle, Lord!
> Not long life by the fire.[16]

## IV   Divine Comedy

In 1893 Louise's name appeared on two new books: Thomas
William Parsons' verse translation of Dante's *Divine Comedy*;
and *A Roadside Harp*, her third, and best, collection of poems.
For Parsons' translation she supplied a "Memorial Sketch" of the
translator, and Professor Charles Eliot Norton wrote the Preface.[17] Her brief biographical treatment made slight demands upon
her scholarship for it was essentially a warm tribute to a close and
honored friend who, in a less dashing fashion than Henri, vindicated
her conception of the hero. Collaboration with the eminent Norton
dictated that, prudently, she leave analysis to him and confine herself to appreciation.

Parsons' incomplete translation had preceded Longfellow's complete one. In fact, Longfellow had modeled "The Poet" of *Tales of
A Wayside Inn* after his old friend, Parsons. Parsons' achievement
had been estimable, both for verbal felicity and consonance with

the spirit of the original Italian. While Louise admired him for his insight into the richness of the Ages of Faith, she loved him as an ideal of dedicated scholarship. No work-worshiping American, he had deliberately rejected public life and success to devote himself to the cultivation of letters; and he had joyfully effaced himself for over fifty years in translating another's greatness. His whole life corresponded to the standards which she had enunciated in "The Precept of Peace": *"la sainte indifférence"* and "the habitually relaxed grasp."[18] He attended Boston Latin School, but did not graduate. He entered Harvard Medical School; yet took no degree. He became a dentist, only to practice briefly and intermittently. Obviously, he did not "covet the game at all."

Louise had spent many hours with Parsons both in Wayland and Scituate; and, once relieved of the obeisance due from her as a collaborator of Norton, she wrote better appreciations elsewhere of Parsons' "moral enthusiasm of fifty-five years . . . done at leisure and by liking," in a follow-up article printed in the *Atlantic* of June, 1894 ("A Poet's Dante"[19]), and a still better verse memorial "T.W.P. 1819–1892," in the quatrains which Parsons had preferred to Dante's terza rima:

> Look not on Fame, but Peace; and in a bower
> Receive at last her fulness *[sic]* and her power:
> Nor wholly, pure of heart!
> Forget thy few, who would be where thou art.[20]

## V  A Roadside Harp

Louise's retrospective judgment of *A Roadside Harp,* her third collection, might seem low: "don't waste your time on *A Roadside Harp*. All that is best in it . . . is in *Happy Ending*."[21] Actually, the slender harp-impressed volume has an integrity and a sustained quality found in none of her other collections of poems. *Happy Ending* (1909), intended as *summa* and swan song, lacks its organic unity; and this appraisal is even truer of the posthumously revised edition of 1927. *Songs at the Start* and *The White Sail* were wing exercises for which *A Roadside Harp* is consummating flight, but it includes the cream of *White Sail* (except "Tarpeia") and the "London" and "Oxford Sonnets." Besides the exquisite "Alexandriana," *A Roadside Harp* introduces the best of her

nature lyrics and some of the finest examples of her religious verse. Yet over all there hangs an autumnal valedictory mist, as though she sensed an approaching finale to her role as poet. Here, along with an improved reworking of "The Wild Ride," are her most characteristic chevalier songs: "The Knight Errant," "The Kings," and "The Vigil-at-Arms," by all of which she was to become a standard feature of poetry anthologies into the 1930's. As a triad, these meet the test of time, consonant in theme, diction, imagery, and rhythm, tautened with a defiance of defeat perceived as impending and ineluctable.

A strange, but superbly sustained sonnet that has occasioned some confusion in the collection is "Friendship Broken." Some have misinterpreted it as evidence of irreparably ruptured friendship with Grace Denslow, but these interpreters have overlooked evidence of the Guiney-Denslow intimacy even while Louise was abroad and the fact that, subsequently, Louise fondly dedicated *The Secret of Fougereuse* to Grace. However, brief alienation was probably forced upon the pair by parent Denslow's refusal to allow his daughter to accept Louise's intended dedication of *Brownies and Bogles*. The consistently maintained *duello* image in the sonnet is simply characteristic of Guiney's chevalier metaphor.

> We chose the faint chill morning, friend and friend,
> Pacing the twilight out beneath an oak,
> Soul calling soul to judgment; and we spoke
> Strange things and deep as any poet penned,
> Such truth as never truth again can mend,
> Whatever art we use, what gods invoke;
> It was not wrath, it made not strife nor smoke:
> Be what it may, it had a solemn end.
> Farewell, in peace. We of the selfsame throne
> Are foemen vassals; pale astrologers,
> Each a wise skeptic of the other's star.
> Silently, as we go our ways alone,
> The steadfast sun, whom no poor prayer deters,
> Drew high between us his majestic bar.[22]

If the Romanticism of "Friendship Broken" is uppermost, the

"Alexandriana" are so authentically Classical in form and in controlled sentiment that not a few critics praised them as superb translations of Greek originals! In a letter to Herbert E. Clarke (January
18, 1894), Louise confessed the hoax: "The 'Alexandriana' are all
jokes, each of them founded on the master-joke that I don't know
omicron from omega, . . . However, they caught several very learned
fish over here. And Dr. Garnett likes 'em: which is glory."[23] But
the real glory lies in such lines from the "Alexandriana" as the haunting
refrain of "A Friend's Song for Simoisius": "Alas, alas, that one
inexorable thing"; or in the Sapphic images of "Charista Musing"
on the marge of a sunny cornfield "Like the sheaves, in beautiful
Doric yellow clad to the ankle."[24]

Guiney's elegiac note had always struck the right minor key, but
in *A Roadside Harp* it is at its saddest-sweetest. Number II of the
"Alexandriana" molds its six lines into the chaste simplicity of a
stele at Marathon:

> Gentle Grecian passing by,
> Father of thy peace, am I;
> Wouldst thou now, in memory,
> Give a soldier's flower to me,
> Choose the standard named of yore
> Beautiful Worth-dying-for,
> That shall wither not, but wave
> All the year above my grave.[25]

The epitaph, "Florentin," also reveals how high her poetry had risen
from the personal to the universal in its lament for lost youth:

> Heart all full of heavenly haste, too like
>     the bubble bright
> On loud little water floating half of an
>     April night,
> Fled from the ear in music, fled from the eye
>     in light,
> Dear and stainless heart of a boy! No sweeter
>     thing can be
> Drawn to the quiet center of God who is
>     our sea:
> Whither, thro' troubled valleys, we also
>     follow thee.[26]

Among the nature and religious lyrics, the sensitivity to change

prevails but with a new poignancy. Even in the buds of promise, spring's beauty unfolds ironic prophecy of the autumn to come:

> April is sad, as if the end she knew,
> The maple's misty red, the willow's gold
> Face-deep in nimble water, seem to hold
> In hope's own water their autumnal hue.[27]

In "Athassel Abbey," the ivied ruins repeat the moral of mutability in the broken rhythm of their mossy arches, while the wind sighs sermons from a crumbled pulpit:

> But I am wind that passes
> In ignorant wild tears,
> Uplifted from the grasses,
> Blown to the void of years,
>
> Blown to the void, yet sighing
> In thee to merge and cease,
> Last breath of beauty dying,
> Of sanctity, of peace.[28]

"A Talisman" distills the essence of renunciation in a classical compactness reminiscent of Walter Savage Landor, but it does so without the esthete's self-sufficiency:

> Take temperance to thy breast,
> While yet is the hour of choosing,
> An arbitress exquisite
> Of all that shall thee betide;
> For better than fortune's best
> Is mastery in the using,
> And sweeter than anything sweet
> The art to lay it aside.[29]

## VI *Shades of the Prison House*

Like the images of siege and citadel in "The Knight Errant," "The Vigil-at-Arms," and "The Kings," the metaphors of renunciation in the nature and spiritual songs coalesce into an audible *vale* in *A Roadside Harp*. During its compilation, Louise had obviously begun to face up to the fact that the "tithes" paid to maintain her mother at Auburndale were woefully inadequate. Actually she had acknowledged this before the collection had gone

to press in a reluctant concession to solicitous friends. At their insistence, and with their support, she had already applied for a vacant postmastership in Auburndale. To her embarrassment, the news was circulated by the press. Charles E. L. Wingate, the *Critic* columnist, while wishing her godspeed, found amusement in the spectacle of a poet at the post office: "We have all known Miss Louise Imogen Guiney as one of the bright lights in Boston litera- ture and never imagined that she would turn to any prosaic pursuit. But it is a fact that Miss Guiney's ambition would lead her to a new 'world of letters.'. . . I should not have said 'ambition'; for though Miss Guiney is desirous of the place and will get it, I hope, yet with her temperament it cannot of course be more than an avocation. . . ."[30]

The news spread as far west as Chicago, where the *Sunday Herald* (December 3, 1893) speculated, prophetically, that her well-known St. Bernard would function as deputy in charge of deliveries, that French-Canadians would flock down from Trois Saumons to *"parler"* with the only United States postmaster com- prehending their patois, and that Harvard boys would buy their stamps in Auburndale just to discuss literature across the counter.

Henry Sherman Wyer reacted with a verse epistle in the *Transcript:*

> Our times, indeed, are out of joint,
> When one whom critics all anoint
> Must needs ask Grover to appoint
> Her Queen of Letters.[31]

Against the grain, Louise also had tried to put a good face on the distasteful inevitable. However, there was no concealing her inward dread that her Muse would be crushed among the mail sacks. In October, 1893, after the official wheels had been set in motion, she wrote a bread-and-butter letter to Dr. William Hayes Ward, prime mover among her partisans: "It is all 'thrift, thrift, Horatio.' I gave fair notice to the gods that I was in need of a rich and moribund uncle; none having applied up to date, I must even go to the govern- ment counter for the possible rest of my days. Here's a chance for my pseudo-Muse to prove romantically faithful; but I'll not trust the girl, well as I love her . . . ."[32]

To her principal English correspondent, Herbert E. Clarke she explained: "the author or conspirator of my being deserves a per- petuity of dinners." But, Louise added, "It occurs to me also, in these

my final hours of liberty and loafing, that if the Muse stays where I mean for a while to put her, behind me, it will harm neither herself, me, nor current civilization."[33] The honeymoon with belles lettres was over. The marriage of convenience had begun.

L.I.G., aged 26, 1887.

**LOUISE  IMOGEN  GUINEY**

# At the Mill with Slaves: 1894–97

I    *"Nor wind, nor hail . . ."*

**P**RESIDENT Grover Cleveland, a fellow Union officer who appreciated General Guiney's services to his country, appointed Miss Guiney the postmistress of Auburndale in January, 1894. She assumed her duties late in the month and, by all records, performed them well. During her term the office showed a profit, was renovated efficiently, and was harmoniously managed by an expanded staff. Any awkwardness which Louise had anticipated in toting sales or in handling money orders vanished in the grinding experience of eleven and, sometimes, fourteen hours a day "engrossed in profane affairs."[1] Her health suffered, of course; and her Muse was "scared off."[2] But, if not poetry, she wrote extensively during her tenure. Maximizing the late evening hours and the weekends, she produced the best of her essays and literary criticism. In just listing her works during this period (1894–97), one is amazed at her energy, and one wonders why she did not collapse earlier than the breakdowns of 1895 and 1897.

Unquestionably, her exhaustion derived mostly from a cruel blow administered by the Auburndale community shortly after she had assumed office. The "American Nativism" which had maddened a Charlestown mob into burning an Ursuline convent in 1834 flared once again in Auburndale. The town was only "Ten Miles Out" of Boston (as Louise frequently headed her letters); but the "Irish Need Not Apply" signs which had begun to disappear in the city still spelled consensus policy in the rural backwaters. The sight of the gentle Hibernian-Catholic lady behind the government grille alarmed local protectionists with the threat of a papal takeover! Because the postmaster's salary depended largely on a percentage of stamp sales in pre-Civil Service days, they organized a town boycott of the post office to drive her out.

Happily, the fair play of Americans generally came to Louise's defense. Leading citizens in Auburndale and across the country

protested the outrage to a patriot's daughter and a cultured young
lady, and orders for stamps inundated the Auburndale Post Office.
Professor Arlo Bates of Massachusetts Institute of Technology
spoke for the enlightened: "There has never before come to my
personal knowledge any instance of persecution so intolerant, so
outrageous, so utterly without a shadow of justification . . . . A
young lady of highest character, of rich and unusual gifts, of perfect official rectitude,—the daughter of a brave and patriotic officer
in the Union Army,—is being hounded out of her means of livelihood
by a company of narrow-minded and violent fanatics, simply on
account of her faith. The thing would be incredible were it not so
actual."[3]

Genuine Americanism won the day, for the boycott was smothered
by the cloud of shame thickening over Auburndale. The post office
registered a profit; but Louise, understandably, was wounded. To
become a *cause célèbre* was anathema to her nature, but to find
her naturally optimistic faith in human nature challenged was more
painful still. But she made no public defense then or when President
McKinley reappointed her in 1897. Even in her private correspondence she hardly referred to the episode. One letter of the period
is exceptional; and, considering its confidential nature to Dora
Sigerson (to explain Louise's coming summer's leave of absence),
it is the mildest of indictments under the circumstances:

News! news! I am going to England again this summer on a brief leave of
absence from the august P.O. authorities . . . . I have had a baddish throat
and head most of the winter, and attribute it to Figures and the Public
Eye, two items which I love not in any wise . . . . The fuss about my office,
I regret to say, absurd as it seems, was no myth, and gave me great worry.
Auburndale is a town populated with retired missionaries, and bigots of
small intellectual calibre . . . . Well, I had some rather rough sailing, thanks
purely to my being a Catholic, . . . I am somewhat broken in now, and
somewhat broken up, too! and ready to forget for a couple of months that
I was ever out of Arcady, or am ever likely to leave it again. Please, don't
say anything of the matter: it is incidental, and must pass.[4]

Work, not recrimination, had been her anodyne during these
painful, but productive, days. Between assuming office and taking the
leave of absence announced to Dora Sigerson, Louise had published
two articles in *Atlantic Monthly,* one in *Catholic World,* another
in *The Chap-Book,* two more for her former publisher of *Wide*

*Awake,* besides three new books: *A Little English Gallery,*[5] "Martha Hilton" in *Three Heroines of New England Romance,*[6] and the Preface to the first complete American edition of Rossetti's *The House of Life*—and all the while she was sustaining her mounting correspondence with literary figures on both sides of the Atlantic.

The Rossetti volume appeared in 1894 under the imprint of Copeland and Day, an offshoot of the Pre-Raphaelite medievalism which had involved Louise in the circle of Cram and his close associate, Bertram Grosvenor Goodhue.[8] Louise's competent prefatory note, like much of her subsequent editing, was unsigned.[9] The short, bouncy biography of Martha Hilton, the New Hampshire Cinderella, was one of a trio of sketches gathered under the title of *Three Heroines of New England Romance* by Harriet Prescott Spofford, the editor, who also contributed the initial story of Priscilla Alden.[10] Alice Brown had written the story of Agnes Surriage, the fisher-maid of Marblehead who married Sir Harry Frankland. But Louise, who had already shown her response to Cavaliers and a corresponding repugnance for Victorian stuffiness, had the best of the material and the most of the fun; for her subject, Martha Hilton (the scullery siren who captured the eye and the hand of the two richest nabobs in the colony), had "the aroma of sex" distressingly absent from the Tudor Exhibition. With humor and insight that eschewed fairy tale and Horatio Alger moral alike, Louise made the parvenu "Lady Wentworth" dance radiantly across pages meant to edify girl readers. Melville had to voyage to the Marquesas to meet Fayaway, but Louise found her in old Portsmouth. Success was the lady, not her marital careers.

## II   *Personal Portraits*

*A Little English Gallery* must have embarrassed President Seelye of Smith College who had found Miss Guiney's qualifications deficient in English literature, for the work evinced what Emily Dickinson called "the phosphorescence of learning,"[11] not just the block-building facts of biography.[12] Collectively, the half dozen figures delineated reaffirmed Louise's devotion to neglected merit and her insight into "the great meanings in minor things": Lady Danvers (1561–1627), mother of George Herbert and dear friend of John

Donne; George Farquhar (1667–1707), author of *The Recruiting Officer* and *The Beaux' Stratagem;* Topham Beauclerk (1739–80) and Bennet Langton (1741–1800), favorite companions of Doctor Johnson and charter members, in 1764, of the famous "Club"; William Hazlitt (1778–1830) and Henry Vaughan (1621–95).

*A Little English Gallery* is the acme of literary appreciation, for it is genuinely warm in tone despite its scholarly discernment. Louise's long suit was that very "faculty of admiration" which Maurice Baring thought indispensable to true greatness and, finding it lacking in Leo Tolstoi, had regretfully denied the eminent Russian election to the first rank. This positive spirit (the antithsis to what Louise later designated as "Wilful Sadness in Literature"[13]) makes the portraits in her *Gallery* glow with sympathy and love. For, however fixed and exacting, her standards of judgments forbade reduction of literary criticism to nit-picking or to pedantic minutiae. The style of the essays matches her viewpoint. It has a brightness and intimacy—her obvious erudition notwithstanding—peculiar to her own genius and sadly wanting in the ponderous Germanic models then being imported into American universities for fatal emulation by emergent doctoral candidates.

Lady Danvers herself was no writer, but she was so generous as a patron of letters that her "every step jostled a Muse."[14] Beauclerk and Langton, amateur scholars and conversationalists in the sparkling circle of Johnson, Goldsmith, and Boswell, were distinguished by their admiration of the great Doctor: "Gay Heart and Gentle Heart, who drove his own blue-devils away with their idolatrous devotion." When Beauclerk (of the flashing, liquid Stuart eye) died at forty-one, Johnson mourned him blackly: "I would walk to the extent of the diameter of the earth to save him."[15] Langton lived to sit beside the dying Johnson and to hold his hand until the end. Both Beauclerk and Langton had recognized a man in Johnson for what he did; Louise recognized the man in them for what they were: rejectors of public careers for an enduring private friendship.

Farquhar appealed to Guiney strongly because, "on a fund of grief," he enriched the late Restoration stage "with a legacy of perpetual merriment."[16] Her treatment reveals an extensive knowledge of English comedy of manners and a sensitive appreciation of the galaxy that was Vanbrugh, Congreve, and Wycherley. But

Farquhar stood out among them. He matched their vivacity and grace, but he transcended the heartlessness of their sophistication. She assumed no holier-than-thou stance toward the libertinism of the age, but she lauded the singular tenderness that overran Farquhar's prompter's book and the unsmirking gaiety of his characters. His rogues are "merely roguish," not villainous.[17] His heroines, like Sylvia of *The Recruiting Officer,* "gallop all the morning after a hunting horn, and all the evening after a fiddle."[18] And, admittedly, she found no problem identifying with him who "did not fulfill himself" by following an "out-going fashion" instead of an "incoming one."[19]

The two longest, and best, essays of *A Little English Gallery* are those about Hazlitt and Vaughan. Each had appeared previously in magazine articles: "William Hazlitt, A Character Study," in *Catholic World,* in January, 1894, as she was commencing her duties as postmistress;[20] and "Henry Vaughan, the Silurist" in *Atlantic Monthly* the following May.[21] Both subjects had a special appeal for her; and Vaughan, whose grave at Llansantffread, Wales, she was instrumental in restoring in 1895, became the focus of numerous articles from her pen during the remainder of her life, as well as a consuming project for a definitive biography planned in collaboration with Miss Gwenllian Morgan of Brecon, Wales.

Louise liked to think of herself as "Hazlitt's child." It was an early compliment which T. W. Parsons had paid her, and she treasured it almost as much as Robert Louis Stevenson's praise of her verses.[22] Hazlitt and Louise Guiney were kin of the heart; both were fighters and verbal virtuosi. Her pilgrimage to Hazlitt's grave in Soho had been family reunion in 1890, and her essay of 1894-95 was another tribute. To be sure, she could not claim detachment in this latest portrait of her "dear and battling spirit," anymore than one can disassociate bias from love or admiration. She had covered the range of his works, as well as his eccentricities, from *Principles of Human Action* to *Liber Amoris.* She could smile at his dependence on his wife for amicably preparing the divorce settlement to facilitate his infatuation with the impossible Sarah Walker. She was ardently Catholic, whereas Hazlitt, a professed Unitarian, was notoriously anti-Romish. She was quintessentially humanist and sophisticated, while he—for all his bootstrap erudition—still retained his villageous mien. But his manhood was compelling: "the only man of

letters in England who dared openly to stand by the French Revolution . . . and who had the magnanimity never to turn his back upon its child and champion."[23] For, like her, he was a rugged, intransigent individualist.

She acknowledged that Hazlitt had no genius for proportion. He loved to digress, for refreshment, in the intriguing byways of incandescent imagination; and she admitted that he fell short of constructive criticism. But he had an insatiable appetite for experience ("the beer and beef of life") that made him "the most ingenuous and agreeable egotist . . . outside of the seventeenth century." The power of his infinitely variable diction—now splendid, now sumptuous; now blunt and crushing as a Saxon mace— derived from his moral earnestness. He illustrated Ruskin's dictum that "No right style was ever founded save out of sincere heart." This style may have cost him his manners, but it preserved his conviction. He took his cue straight from nature, with "a fine barbaric cocksureness."[24] Because he never sold himself, he became "the visionary of humanity, the fool of virtue"[25]—"the outrider of universal freedom" in a day of coarseness and tyranny, bequeathing mankind "a memory like a lodestar, and a name which is a toast to be drunk standing."[26]

Louise, who proposed the toast as finale, could hardly join those standing to drink it. For, as "Hazlitt's child," she was hailing herself, so like him: "a great pedestrian" from childhood; a hater of schoolmasters "on principle"; one who dwelt not "with althoughs and neverthelesses"; one who "lusted like Sir Thomas Browne to find the great meanings of minor things" and who depended so entirely upon memory that "those who knew him best say that he never took notes."

Henry Vaughan received similar loving-and-scholarly treatment in a sixty-five-page essay, for subject and author were again "naturals" for each other. Far from the crowd in willing withdrawal; childlike in spirit and organically knit to the beauties of nature; loyal to dispossessed tradition; and religious to the core, they were spiritually brother and sister. Louise found in Vaughan the epitome of her ideals: Jacobite Cavalier and Christian mystic; and Vaughan found in her his most simpatico apologist.

As in her appreciation of Hazlitt, a meticulous scholarship checked the ardors of the enthusiast. She combed the available Vaughan texts,

sifting the variations of old printers. She immersed herself em-
pathically in his "Siluria" until she could evoke the mood, as well
as the milieu, of Wales. Her researches into his contemporaries
added another dimension to the total perspective constructed for his
appreciation—particularly marked in the comparative quotations
paralleling the similarities and differences of Vaughan and Herbert.
Yet no pedantry marred her scholarship.

Louise's rediscovery of Vaughan enabled her to undo the "epic
blunder" committed by Chamber's *Cyclopedia* in pigeonholing
Vaughan as a "gloomy sectarian." Far from being pessimistic, her
Vaughan was a genuinely Christian poet who brought the beauty
of religion to readers who found Richard Crashaw too hectic,
William Cowper too terrifying, or Frederick Faber too saccharine.
"The nimbus is about his laic song," she wrote. "When he talks of
moss and rocks, it is as if they were incorporated into the spiritual."[27]
Vaughan's was the last vision of the Old Faith, filtered through
the veil of the pristine Anglicanism which had composed the Book of
Common Prayer and translated the King James Bible. With him,
orthodoxy had not yet evaporated into pantheism or into theological compromises with Rationalism. He kept the heart of a child, whether riding to his doctor's house calls in the countryside or kneeling in
wayside chapels. Until Guiney's time, he had become a *curiosus*
of antiquarians, quaint, if not quite uncouth.

The full-length treatment which Louise planned for Vaughan
never materialized. Her prolonged, extensive researches, pushed to
the verge of publication, were preempted by the appearance in 1903
of Professor George Saintsbury's definitive work about the minor
Carolian poets. But she had done more than recover Vaughan's
neglected grave and reputation; she had erected, with a long suc-
cession of articles and editions, her own unique monument to "one
of the best and sweetest minds of the seventeenth century."[28]
Besides the initial essay in *A Little English Gallery,* she published, in 1902, a closely edited collection of Vaughan's prose *(The
Mount of Olives and Primitive Holiness),* and in later years four
scholarly essays: "Lovelace and Vaughan: A Speculation," *Catholic
World* (August, 1912); "Milton and Vaughan," *Quarterly* (April,
1914); and, in consecutive *Nation* installments "Henry Vaughan:
Unpublished Letters, With a Commentary" (March 11 and 15,
1915).

*A Little English Gallery* was the kind of literary criticism that American scholarship needed but could not import from either Bonn or Heidelberg. Moreover, their writing also allowed Louise an adjustment to the post-office routine which her Muse could not make. She acknowledged this practical state of affairs in sending an autographed gift copy to Edward A. Church: "Suffer the infliction, by this mail, of a little book wherein I am on my own ground, ... *A Little English Gallery* be your penance, this time. Look on that sort of thing as my literary business in life. The poetry is what I do for fun."[29] Nevertheless, she had to get away from both businesses—post office and prose—for a long respite in England.

### III   *Runaway*

The walking tour of England with Alice Brown in the spring of 1895 was, however, good business. The two young ladies had just co-edited *A Summer in England,* a *vademecum* for the Women's Rest Tour Association, destined for reeditions until the turn of the century; and their clientele deserved some revised notes. The pair headed straight for Wales and "Siluria." They found Vaughan's grave ("occulo irretoro") and, later, contacted Gwenllian Morgan, the Vaughan expert—although Louise, thereafter a regular correspondent in their mutual project, was not to meet Miss Morgan personally until her own permanent removal to England in 1901. Guiney-Brown badgered Sir Edmund Gosse into reluctant concession to their campaign for funding decent restoration of Vaughan's neglected grave at Llansantffread; and they crossed Thomas Hardy's heath in the storm that evoked Louise's poetic response: "Romans in Dorset." At Hazlitt's favorite Pheasant Inn, they toasted "Billie" with his own favorite shandy-gaff, to the frowns of less enthusiastic Americans who read of the "orgy" through the Boston *Herald* and the New York *World.*[30]

But London was still the irresistible capital of Louise's heart. There she met Lionel Johnson, whose name she was to evangelize in the United States: "a calm Virgilian young person, small and silent, with a knowing sidelong smile, pleasant as a bookish fay's."[31] A less impressive, if more formidable literary lion, was Theodore Watts-Dunton: "a funny little Buddha."[32] But, most frequently, she met with Herbert Clarke to exchange literary transatlantica and to

listen to his suggestions for improving her "Oxford" sonnets which
had been aborning since her first visit to the university during her
tour of 1889–91. Now they were completed after renewed visits and
longer strolls in the ivied quadrangles. Seen from the old city wall,
overlooking the spires and towers of Oxford, a thousand pinnacles
("like an angelic army's spurs"[33]) pricked her heart into expression:
"On the Pre-Reformation Churches," "The Old Dial of Corpus,"
"Undertones at Magdalen." Most of these sonnets Clarke approved,
but he cautioned her against the habitual "congestion" that may
have been transmitted to her from reading too much Sidney, Donne,
or Vaughan.[34]

Yet London, itself, where she had taken quarters at 28 Gower
Street, was the main attraction—especially its bustle and freedom.
She was no more Anglophile than when she had resided there with
her mother in 1889–91, for she still missed "Jokes, cold soda, and
the Bird of Freedom."[35] She could spot quicksilver Americans
"a mile down the street by . . . the eternal glint of their humor-loving
eye."[36] She agreed with Hawthorne that England was the utmost
in mundane felicity, "except the population"; and it should be
replaced with a Yankee equivalent by international exchange: half
a million every hundred years.[37] Otherwise, the Strand and High
Holborn were "Paradise enow": "I want to live in Holborn, and on
High Holborn stand, with no hat upon my forehead and no' count-
books in my hand. It is like the very land of Canaan to me, with
never a pole of wire in the streets; never a blockade; never a fat
woman in the 'bus upon your knee, and seven infants clinging to
the straps overhead; never nobody to care nothing if you don't
attend his tuppence-ha'penny Church."[38]

## IV  *Repatriate*

The last line, written to a neighbor, could not but recall Auburn-
dale-of-the-boycott. But Auburndale and its post office also recalled
her, as September's declining sun slanted across the dial like the
finger of conscience. She returned to Boston with Alice Brown,
docking in the harbor for an author's welcome from Fred Holland
Day: "there, on the pier, mounted on a barrel, was young Mr. Day,
Miss Brown's publisher, . . . with the big gold-and-green poster of
her book, *Meadowgrass,* pinned on his breast."[39] But if, indis-

creetly, he had failed to fly her colors also, he was soon making amends to Louise: four titles of hers appeared under his imprint before he suddenly decided to sell his firm on Cornhill—one of these publications *(Lovers' Saint Ruth's and Other Tales)* was rushed into print against her misgivings, and another *(Patrins)* was the most durable of her collections of essays.

Preceding both, however, was the Brown-Guiney collaborative tribute to lately deceased Robert Louis Stevenson.[40] The issue of two hundred and fifty copies was printed for private distribution in 1895 by Copeland and Day. Though both women shared the same idolatry of "R. L. S." and had actively campaigned for erection of his memorial fountain in San Francisco,[41] Alice was credited with the "Study" and Louise with the enveloping "Prelude" and "Postlude." Brown's biographical appreciation, however sincere, was gushingly adulatory; and Louise's "Prelude" also suffered the strains of forced tribute, altogether metrically inconsonant to a requiem calling for deep intonation from the heart.[42] But the "Postlude" (reprinted from *Century Magazine* of March, 1895, and, subsequently, reentitled "Valediction: R.L.S.") would have pleased Stevenson even more than the Guiney verses which he had praised before his death. Characteristically, the work is a Petrarchan sonnet which fittingly accentuated what Stevenson had always stressed: the perennial-positive, soon to become mortared as keystone of her principles of criticism in the Preface to *Carmen,* the essays in *Patrins,* and the "Study" of Mangan:

> When from the vista of the Book I shrink,
> From lauded pens that earn ignoble wage,
> Begetting nothing joyous, nothing sage,
> Nor keep with Shakespeare's use one golden link:
> When heavily my sanguine spirits sink,
> To read too plain on each impostor page
> Only of kings the broken lineage,
> Well for my peace if then on thee I think,
> Louis: our priest of letters, and our knight
> With whose familiar baldric hope is girt,
> From whose young hands she bears the Grail away.
> All glad, all great! Truer because thou wert,
> I am and must be; and in thy known light
> Go down to dust, content with this my day.[43]

*Lovers' Saint Ruth's and Other Tales* only proves what Louise was the first to admit: she had slender endowment for prose fiction. Day had cajoled the manuscript from her, against her wishes; for she regarded it before and after publication as a disaster. To Edward A. Church she protested: "I could weep to see you reading my one book which I heartily dislike! It was fairly dragged out of me, after long solicitation . . . . I mean to head it off from ever going into a second edition."[44] The title page of her personal copy bears this penciled note: "N.B.—This book is NO Good! 1896"[45] The title story, about an ancient shrine become a lovers' rendezvous, incompatibly mixed exposition with narration. The plot (compounded of murder and rape redeemed by fidelity) had a violence and sensationalism precariously melodramatic. Of the other three tales, all lacking inventiveness and fulsomely sentimental, "The Provider" alone showed some merit in a sympathetic depiction of poor children in the Dublin slums.

Guiney's last book to be published in 1895 also came from the presses of Copeland and Day: a small leaflet, entitled *Nine Sonnets Written at Oxford,* for private distribution as Christmas gifts. However slight, it was so handsomely printed by Day and decorated by Bertram Grosvenor Goodhue that, at the William Morris sale of 1901, the Bodleian Library paid a large sum for a single copy on the supposition that it must have come from the Kelmscott Press. Louise's sonnets had profited from her *labor limae* with Herbert Clarke. Poignantly, they underscored the deep attachment that would, ultimately, draw her back to Oxford. "Number IV," for example, recites a rosaried litany of veneration, telling each beaded name with the touch of a Whitman or a Vachel Lindsay:

> Imperial Iffley, Cumnor bowered in green,
> And Templar Santford in the boatman's call,
> And sweet-belled Appleton, and Elsfield wall
> That doth upon adoring ivies lean;
> Meek Binsey; Dorchester where streams convene
> Bidding on graves her solemn shadow fall;
> Clear Cassington that soars perpetual;
> Holton and Hampton Poyle, and fanes between:[46]

Number VIII ("A Last View") not only reaffirms the hold that

England and Oxford had fastened on Guiney but reminds the reader
of the sacrifice entailed in her return to the drudgery of Auburndale:

> Sweet, on those dim long-dedicated walls,
> Silver as rain the frugal sunshine falls:
> Slowly sad eyes resign them, bound afar.
> Dear Beauty, dear Tradition, fare you well,
> And powers that aye aglow in you, impel
> Our quickening spirits from the slime we are.[47]

# Annus Mirabilis: 1897

A LTHOUGH 1896 was the hardest year in her life, it was, miraculously, also the most productive. By the spring of 1897, Louise collapsed under what was then being called "meningitis."[1] The burden of a double life, postmistress and author, had undermined her health. But the result in literary achievement was incontestable. Publication of her Preface to *Carmen,* of the essay collection, *Patrins* (especially its "Wilful Sadness in Literature" and "On the Rabid *versus* the Harmless Scholar"), and of her "Study" of Mangan established her among American professional critics. For, collectively, these publications vindicated her remarks about *A Little English Gallery.* Scholarship was "her business" in life.[2]

## I   Carmen

By any standards, *Carmen* was a triumph, in format and contents. A deluxe edition of Mérimée's classic short story, it had been bound in white and gold by Little, Brown and Company, and illustrated excitingly by Louise's collaborator on *Brownies and Bogles* and *Three Heroines of New England Romance:* the versatile Edmund H. Garrett, who also supplied the translation of Mérimée's original.[3] Few books are best known for their prefaces, save George Bernard Shaw's legendary ones; but Louise's "Memoir" is another such instance. This stature was acknowledged by the *Bookman's* prompt review: "It can be said of few books that we like them the better for the preface, and of fewer still that we cherish them for the sake of the preface, as we do in this case." The Boston *Advertiser* chose to laud the nice integration of the work: "If translator, illustrator and essayist had deliberately combined to create new enthusiasts and admirers of the Frenchman, they could hardly have chosen or worked more subtly and wisely."[4]

The "Memoir" was a triumph in a special sense for Louise. Adhering to Prosper Mérimée's Gallic concision in her critique, she suppressed an innate aversion to all that his Naturalism rep-

resented. Actually, she had written her evaluation four years earlier, during the "French period" of her translations of Alexander Dumas, Emile Augier, and Casimir Delavigne; but she had withheld it from submission until asked to collaborate with Garrett in the Little, Brown edition of 1897: "The truth is, I dislike Mérimée *in toto;* but I tried to be just."[5] For Mérimée, by virtue of his ennui and his cynicism, was the antithesis of her beloved "R. L. S.," "begetting nothing joyous, nothing sage."[6] Nevertheless, her "Memoir" concedes him full measure of admiration for his artistry. His symmetry becomes hers, restraining her native tendency toward "congestion" (observed by Clarke) and matching his own lucid epigrams in the accommodation of style to subject: "He has a style of gold and steel . . . . His details bite in like an etching. He deals in an economy both of emotions and words, and in a sort of short-hand diction of consummate elegance, informed with wonderful terseness, austerity, and compression. He did not write for the mob. . . . There is nothing exaggerated or superfluous in Mérimée's work . . . founded on essentials, on the lasting and stern generalities, and . . . deep into the bed-rock of human nature."[7]

Unquestionably, Louise's judgment was influenced by her knightly concept of the self-sacrificing hero and by her own life of grinding toil that so sharply contrasted to Mérimée's prodigal indolence. Certainly, Mérimée, the sybaritic *flaneur,* contradicted her classical sense of the responsibilities of high art. Literature, simply put, was to Louise too serious to leave to the *littérateur.* Because Mérimée's cup of cynicism overflowed with negativism, Guiney found him a "callous inscrutable Mephisto," whose aim was "to shock and to vex: the conscious audacity of little minds." Beside his sophisticated, elegant style, Emily Brontë's tumultous style in *Wuthering Heights* was smooth because sincere. To Louise, "With all his gifts, Mérimée lacked 'the material for mental happiness' He was too timid, too restless, . . . too fearful of ridicule and misconception. Something of the feminine-bitter pervaded both his temperament and his talent; a direct inheritance, perhaps from his clever and devoted mother, who gave her boy for motto the satanic talisman: . . . *Remember to mistrust.*"[8]

Louise had riveted "armour gay" onto her "Knight Errant," even at the approach of the Dragon; and she had hailed her "knight elect" as "soul ordained to fail." She was quite incapable, therefore, of

conceiving a great literature not based on faith, hope, or love. Her aspiration for "A short life in the saddle, Lord!/Not long life by the fire" was incompatible with Mérimée's decline on the beaches of Cannes—reading and drawing landscapes until, attended by cats and two ancient British gentlewomen, he died, "weary of art and humanity,"[9] in his sleep. Already in treating Mérimée she had formulated the critical principles sketched in *Goose-Quill Papers* and soon to be consolidated in her dissent from Matthew Arnold in her "Wilful Sadness in Literature":

His fatal disease, . . . was indifferentism. You feel wroth at him that he went out of the world, not like a veteran from the battlefield, but like a girl from the ball-room, in smiling weariness, and without a scar.[10] M. Jules Lemaître considers that a most distinguished attitude toward life! . . . it is the dream of every sophomore before he has begun to think.

A mask is very irritating when its wearer is a man of genius. Unlike Hamlet, who "knew not seems," Prosper Mérimée knew little else; his whole character was encased in reserve one might rightly call ungenerous . . . . The ultimate verdict on "the visionary of humanity, the fool of virtue," is that he is a most blessed person. He is no miser; he has spent his immortal patrimony of energy and faith.[11]

Her appreciation of Gypsy Carmen, however, was another thing: she was a true heroine who espoused death as "an artistic necessity" and who chose it "as a fresh ribbon for her bodice."[12] In her, Guiney recognized the elemental sex force repressed in American letters and only recently stripped bare by French Naturalism—and she praised Mérimée for its honesty, as well as for its art. But, then, this required no deviation from the standards of a woman who had admired Hazlitt for his zest as a trencherman and who had commended Beardsley because he loved to give Solemnity a shock. Andalusian Carmen was only a more flamboyant Martha Hilton. More basically, Guiney's philosophy asserted the goodness of life per se. Only the disfigurement or the rejection of life was base.

## II    *James Clarence Mangan*

Louise may have been among the best analysts of Mérimée, but she could not claim to have introduced him to American readers. With Clarence Mangan, as with Lionel Johnson, it was different. She rescued Mangan from the misty legends of a local Irish reputation

and made startling assertions in his name. She had learned of his gutter genius during her first visit to Ireland and her acquaintance with the Sigersons of Dublin. She had presented him to American audiences in an *Atlantic* article in 1891.[13] What that article had sketched, she presented fully in a one-hundred-page "Study" prefacing her edition of *James Clarence Mangan: His Selected Poems,* published in May, 1897.[14] The claims were extraordinary, and the validation was impressive.

One of her bent could hardly have failed to respond to Mangan's merits, especially after researches on Mérimée; for the French and Irish authors were absolute opposites. Instead of the trail of unbroken success of Mérimée, Mangan had followed the dark way of the opium eater, from grinding toil as an attorney's copyist to a charity bed in Meath Hospital. Louise's edition of his remarkable poems had required five years of work from conception to completion, and it was achieved in the busiest and hardest period of her life. But such was the poet's hold upon her that she risked a physical breakdown and jeopardized *Patrins* to conclude the edition. The day-by-day account may be followed in her letters (1895–97) in which she is now hopeful, now despairing. A letter of September, 1896, to William Van Allen recapitulates the problems: "I am under a grinding vow to edit Clarence Mangan and Henry Vaughan (two most difficult and interminable JOBS ... ), write some short papers for the *Atlantic,* and get a book of little good-for-nothing essays *[Patrins]* ready for the printers .... If ever I get to Paradise, I have a stipulation: that I shall play games, in the open air, for ever and ever."[15]

When finished, however, her edition of Mangan's selected poems won kudos immediately from the poet's biographer, D.J.O'Donoghue of Dublin: "the crème de la crème of Mangan's verse, ... on the whole I think nothing better if as good has ever been written of Mangan."[16] Though Louise welcomed the compliment and took greater satisfaction in the knowledge that she had rectified the slight mention of Mangan in Allibone's *Dictionary of Authors* and his scandalous omission from the *Encyclopaedia Brittannica,* she modestly restained her summary evaluation of him: "He has been, for a half-century, wandering on the dark marge of Lethe. It will not do, as yet to startle him with gross applause. Otherwise, his gratified editor would like to repeat, ... the gallant words with

which Schumann once began a review of the young Chopin: "Hats off, gentlemen, a genius!"[17]

That Mangan was a genius Louise never doubted. Quick to champion slighted worth, she was nothing if not enthusiastically involved in his cause. Yet, responsibly, she avoided the cultist's hyperbole. Mangan was not a near-great because he had lived in a garret or because he had resorted to drugs; he had achieved in spite of both. Still, her opening pages suggest a Romantic suscepti-bility to the myths of bohemia, if not quite a morbid fascination with the eccentric:

Apollo has a class of might-have-beens whom he loves; poets bred in melancholy places, . . . with thwarted growth and thinned voices; . . . Man-gan's is such a memory, captive and overborne. It may be unjust to lend him the epitaph of defeat, for he never strove at all. One can think of no other, in the long disastrous annals of English literature, cursed with so monotonous a misery, so much hopelessness and stagnant grief. He had no public; he was poor, infirm, homeless, loveless; . . . the cruel necessities of labor sapped his dreams from a boy; . . . the demon of opium, then the demon of alcohol, pulled him under, body and soul, despite a persistent and heartbreaking struggle, and he perished ignobly in his prime.[18]

Despite Louise's fascination she kept Rosalind's common sense in the romantic Forest of Arden. Mangan was simply not bred for con-ventional happiness. He was ineffably unhappy and poured his lone-liness into verse that occasionally transcended his personal malaise. Nor did she seek a chemical explanation for the fantastical world opened to his imagination. Interestingly, her analysis of his hand-written manuscripts convinced her also that they lacked the tell-tale marks of the alcoholic which gossip labeled him; his face, never-theless, (even in the posthumous portrait by Burton) did suggest the drugged "alabaster shine" that had characterized the better-known Thomas De Quincey. Sensibly, Louise maintained that it was pathologically impossible for a man to be drunkard and addict simultaneously.

She conceded, however, that Mangan had unquestionably beheld Xanadu visions, for these are confirmed in his own confession: "The Gorgon's head, the triple-faced hell-dog, the handwriting on Belshazzar's palace-wall, . . . all are *bagatelles* beside the phantas-magoria which haunt my brain, and blast my eyes."[19] Yet his genius lay not in these, but in his passage through them without

foundering on the rocks of satanic bestiality or pseudo-mysticism. While his body paid the exacted toll of deprivation and drugs, his spirit stayed untouched; and, for a starveling bard, he miraculously preserved his sense of humor. She knew that his polyglot pretensions were "pure blague," although his "translations" from the Persian had taken in the leading Orientalists of the day. She chuckled over the gigantic hoax of his "Ottoman Proverbs" and the audacious nomenclature of his sources: Berri-Abel, Bham-Booz-eel, Ben Daood. The only victory which he ever won was most impressive because he won it over himself, his hardships, and his melancholia.

A true Irishman, Mangan could not resist anything so specifically national as a political opinion. His ballads, squandered on ephemeral journals or sung by cracked tenors in squalid pubs, served the Young Ireland party well. Many of these were "middling verse," turgid with nostalgic patriotism; but there were the brilliant, still memorable exceptions: "My Dark Rosaleen," "Kathleen Ny-Houlahan," "Leather Away with the Wattle, O" and "At Tarah Today." "Dark Rosaleen," particularly, had the authentic bardic echo of the Gaelic original; but Mangan, for all his dabbling into German and Persian, knew no Gaelic. Even his Orientalism had been picked up second-hand from Johann Herder and August and Friedrich von Schlegel during long hours of keeping warm in the Trinity College Library and in the Map Room of the Ordnance Society.

The refrain, lushly musical and hauntingly recurrent, was the hallmark of his style. Undoubtedly, he had aped it first from Samuel Taylor Coleridge; but, with his own more uninhibited sensationalism, he fashioned it into a flexible instrument for transmission to Edgar Allan Poe and to W. S. Gilbert, both also verbal virtuosi on the order of Paganini performers. When Miss Guiney analyzed one of Mangan's poems, "Metempsychosis" (allegedly derived from Klauter-Katowski's "Popular Songs of the German"), she concluded that here was "the exhumed precursor of the Mikado."[20] Her claims for Mangan's influence on Poe were less conjectural; for the successive sonorous lines of Mangan's "The Karamanian Exile," for example, could easily be attributed to the Poe of "Al Aaraaf,"—as could the curious diction and hypnotizing repetitions. The prosodic evolution of Poe's "Lenore," from "A Paean" of 1831, to "Ulalume" in 1847, strongly suggested the intermediary influence of Mangan on the notorious American buc-

caneer. She conceded, fairly, that Poe's plundering career was "a patrician aggressiveness never to be confounded with common theft," for he touched nothing that he did not adorn.[21] But she cautioned lest Poe, the superior artist, be anointed to reign also in the little realm of the dispossessed Mangan whom he resembled so much: in physique, literary endowment, kindred obsessions, and common fate.

There were differences, too, between Mangan and Poe, those essential differences which she had contrasted in Stevenson and Mérimée: "Poe, with his manifold gifts . . . was 'of the highest order of the seraphim illuminati who sneer.' He nursed grudges and hungered for homage; he was seldom so happy as in a thriving quarrel. Mangan was a pattern of sweet gratitude and deference, and left his art to prosper or perish, as Heaven should please."[22] Mangan's true kinsmen were Emily Brontë, Hartley Coleridge, and Thomas Lovell Beddoes: lavish in promise, defrauded in life, neglected in recognition. Knights of the pen, their lance may have quivered in the hide of the Dragon success; but it never broke. They were heroes first, and writers after—"footnotes to history," perhaps, like M. Henri, in a darker *bocage;* but, for Louise, theirs were names to be toasted standing.

### III   Patrins

The critical principles elucidated in *Carmen* and in *James Clarence Mangan* are elaborated and consolidated in *Patrins* (1897).[23] Louise's dedication to Bliss Carman explains the title: "A *patrin,* according to *Romano Lavo-Lil,* is a Gypsy trail: handfuls of leaves or grass cast by the Gypsies on the road, to denote, to those behind, the way which they have taken." This final collection of her essays was composed of selections from ten previous years of contributions to the *Atlantic Monthly,* the *Chap-Book,* the *Independent,* the *Catholic World,* and the Providence *Journal.* Two of the inclusions ("An Open Letter to the Moon" and "On Teaching One's Grandmother How to Suck Eggs") had been reprinted from *Goose-Quill Papers.* Three of these essays, particularly when combined with the ten verse "Colloquies" of *Happy Ending,* enable the reader to follow the trail of her development as a critic: "On the Rabid *versus* the Harmless Scholar," "Wilful Sadness in Literature," and "An Inquirendo." The book

appeared on the stalls within two weeks after the publication of her
*Mangan,* a feat evidencing that she was certainly the busiest postmaster writing in the United States—and the quality of the essays
also suggested that she was a singular literary critic for a postmaster
and an eminent one in the field of letters more broadly considered.

"On the Rabid *versus* the Harmless Scholar," with its equation
of leisure with culture, may point toward Miss Guiney's ultimate
removal to England in 1901 and to her subsequent apologia for
expatriation made in "On a Preference for Living in England."[24]
In the hustling America to which she had returned in 1895,
the essay was tantamount to heresy because of the national religion of work. She indicted taxing labors because they prohibited a
right representation to pleasure. Like liberty, joy was worth dying for
in the republic of letters. What Emerson had insufficiently accommo-
dated among his marks of the American scholar, Louise headlined in
hers: lightness, gusto, even casualness.

The "noxious variety of student" was ceaselessly activist, sub-
sidized by some "Facts Foundation." Restless amid the detachment
of contemplation, he could never let well enough alone but had to be
ever "fearfully foraging with intent to . . . govern an academy" or
running in squads after Anglo-Saxon or that "blatant beast,"
comparative mythology.[25] For Louise, the mark of true learning
(qualitative rather than quantitative) was not sweat or midnight oil.
Taste knew when to shuck "all superfluous effort," and acquired its
mental stock "secretly, decently, pleasantly." Sometimes, wisely,
scholarship diffused not knowledge, she affirmed, but "the more
needful scorn of knowledge" when learning degenerated into mere
information. Louise, accordingly, feared the university where
things were taught with great vigor; for by her standards the main
business of the scholar was "to live gracefully, without mental passion,
and to get off alone into a corner for an affectionate view of creation."
What a loss to mankind it would have been, she observed, had that
wonderful wastrel Laurence Sterne made his sentimental journey
to measure the spandrels of Rouen cathedral! Maria by the brookside,
or even the dead ass, had taught him more. For the truth was that
"very few can be trusted with an education." The best thing, therefore, that Louise could say about a savant was that he was not only
"unformidable" but that he reminded everyone of "a distant or
deceased uncle."[26] Such a scholar had not been ruined for this

world, or any other, by initiation into the dubious minutiae of recondite arcana.

"Wilful Sadness in Literature" also accentuates the positive without slinking out of the race for experience. It acknowledges the tragic and the terrible; it eschews only the morbid and the mean. Louise had defined her position by commending Matthew Arnold for his decision to withdraw *Empedocles on Etna* from circulation: "Nothing in Mr. Arnold's career did him more honor than that fine scrupulousness leading him to decry his dramatic masterpiece as too mournful, too unfruitful of the cheer and courage which it is the business of poets to give to the world."[27]

Yet she acknowledged that art could not evade the problem of evil: "Sadness which is impersonal, reluctantly uttered, and adjusted, in the utterance, to the eternal laws, is not so. It is well to conceal the merely painful, as did the Greek audiences and the masters of their drama. That critic would be crazy, or excessively sybaritic, who would bar out the tragic from the stage, studio, the orchestra, or the library shelf. Melancholy, indeed, is inseparable from the highest art. We cannot wish it away; but we can demand a mastery of it in the least, as well as in the greatest. . . . "[28] By their very moderation, the Greeks had distilled awe and piety from the crucible of Oedipus' and Orestes' agonies. The dark tragedies of Shakespeare and his contemporaries had compelled men toward thoughtfulness, not self-pity; and Johnson's and Browning's conquest of melancholia had made them great, as well as lovable. Truly great writers, who had overcome adversity, could ask encouragingly: "What had I on earth to do/With the slothful, with the mawkish, the unmanly?"[29] Profound pathos derives from seemly abstinences, but "Too much" destroys the authority of its mystery. Lear's heartbreaking climax is properly confined to a dying commonplace, almost grotesque: "Pray you, undo this button."

Withal, Louise was not hostile to the swelling current of Naturalism. She did call Mary Wilkins Freeman "a sordid Aeschylus,"[30] but she wrote a fine appreciation of Harold Frederic in the *Book Buyer*[31] and defended the bleakness in Edith Wharton's *Ethan Frome* in an incisive letter to the Reverend J. J. Burke.[32] Her standards of the role of the artist's responsibilities may have been austerely classical, but her judgments of persons were charitably catholic. "Wilful Sadness in Literature" was a code—not a condemnation.

Nor did the twin Horatian canons of *docere et placere* postulate
suffocation of self by tradition. The nice equation between the two
components of art finds expression in the verse parallels which her
"Colloquies" afford for the critical principles pervading "On the
Rabid *versus* the Harmless Scholar" and "Wilful Sadness in
Literature":

III.  The Poet's Chart

. . . . . . .

Turn from another's track
Whether for gain or lack,
Love but thy natal right.
Cease to follow withal,
Though on thine up-led feet
Flakes of the phosphor fall.
Oracles overheard
Are never again for thee,
Not at a magian's knee
Under the hemlock tree,
Burns the illumining word.

. . . . . . . .

Neither from sires nor sons,
Nor the delivered ones,
Holy, invoked with awe.
Rather, dredge the divine
Out of thine own poor dust,
Feebly to speak and shine.

Schools shall be as they are:
Be thou truer, and stray
Alone, intent, and away,
In a savage wild to obey
Some dim primordial star.

IV.  Of The Golden Age

Recall for me, recall
The time more true and ample:
The world whereon I trample,
How torturous and small!
Behold, I tire of all.

Once, gods in jewelled mail
Through greenwood ways invited:
There now the moon is blighted,
And mosses long and pale
On lifeless cedars trail.

Child keep this good unrest:
But give to thine own story
Simplicity with glory;
To greatness dispossessed,
Dominion of thy breast.

In abstinence and pride,
Thou, who from Folly's boldest
Thy sacred eye withholdest,
Another morn shalt ride
At Agamemnon's side.[33]

## IV   *Restoration, 1897*

The last line of "Wilful Sadness" closed sanguinely: "The May-
pole is up in Bookland." Right or wrong as prophecy, it effected
the proper transition to the sequent essay in *Patrins*, "An Inquirendo
into the Wit and Other Good Parts of His Late Majesty, King

Charles the Second"; for Charles II led England a merry dance for
the twenty-five years of his reign. Louise's life-long affection for
the "Black-bird" Stuart might appear inconsistent with her personal morality or with her views as critic-moralist. But, just as her
probity had nothing of prissiness, her fondness for the misnamed
Merry Monarch had no delusions. She had dubbed him "A King
of Shreds and Patches" in the original *Catholic World* article of
1887.[34] He was still a rogue and a wastrel in 1897, though the
decade's interval had, undoubtedly, deepened her appreciation of
"His Wit and Other Good Parts." He had not changed, of course;
he simply looked better in retrospect, after the suffocating smog of
Puritan righteousness and Victorian dullness: "Whenever I think of
Charles the Second's speech and bearing, and indomitable intelligence, and then of the excellent lady, . . . who now gloriously
reigneth, I pause, and slap my knee for a secret Jacobite."[35]

Louise's target was neither Queen Victoria nor the house of
Hanover-Windsor, for her barbs were aimed at whatever she regarded as the "stuffed-shirt" front of moral smugness attitudinizing
as Mosaic legislator, whether a democrat or an imperialist. Woodrow
Wilson inherited the rebuke when Victoria had been immortalized
by Madame Tussaud, especially after his ministerial-magisterial ap-
parition in London prior to his apotheosis at Versailles.[36] Whatever else Charles lacked, he never had the insolence to accept deifica-
tion. For all its royal trappings, his regime was basically democratic, founded on his own sure sense of fallibility: "It would have
terrified him had one subject in his realm taken him too seriously."

Charles had shown courage at the battle of Worcester and during
the flight to France that followed. He had borne his weary exile
at the court of Louis XIV with equal fortitude. His first acts after
the Restoration of 1660 were "gracious grand-opera things":
amnesty for his enemies, parks for the people, and theaters reopened
in London. Characteristically, he "abolished the statute which had
thoughtfully provided for the roasting of heretics." But, as he
explained to his "deare, deare Sister," Henrietta, he would not
abolish cock-fighting: "I am one of those Bigotts who thinks that
malice is a much greater sinn than a poore frailty of nature."[37]
He restored manners, as well as wit, to officialdom. When Quaker
Penn, armored in ostentatious humility, persisted in wearing his
broad-brim while petitioning a charter, Charles quietly removed his

own feathered hat with the excuse: "Because it has long been the custom here for but one person to remain covered at a time." When Nell Gwynne affected to hurl his baby from a balcony for want of a name for their son, he doffed as he galloped past: "Spare the Earl of Burford!"

Restoration rottenness might eventually provoke every street-corner evangelist in the British Isles to don the mantle of Jeremiah and rail against corruption; but Louise chose to focus on its human sparkle: "There was an astonishing dearth of dull people; the bad and bright were in full blossom, and the good and stupid were pruned away." London was as unlike Boston or Balmoral as possible, and more like the hell which Aucassin had preferred for its "superior social qualities."[38] When a German wife was proposed to Charles for cementing alliances, he rejected the notion firmly: "so dull and foggy."

If that view of German royalty was one bond in their agreement, Louise found another in their mutual love of dogs. She quoted the advertisement which Charles personally placed in *Mercurius Publius* on June 28, 1660, for a lost favorite: "a Black Dog, between a grey hound and a spaniel, no white about him, only a streak on his Brest and Tayl a little bobbed." Louise continued her quotation to afford a fuller insight into the wit of this king questionably dubbed "The Merry Monarch;" "It is His Majesties own Dog, and doubtless was stoln, for the Dog was not born or bred in England, and would never forsake his Master. Whosoever findes him, may acquaint any at Whitehall, for the Dog was better known at Court than those who stole him. Will they never leave robbing His Majesty? Must he not keep a Dog? This Dog's place, (though better than some imagine) is the onely place which nobody offers to Beg."[39]

Charles may have passed into history as "the Merry Monarch" rather than as the keeper of the peace in England or as the architect of Britannia's supremacy on the seas; but Louise probed beneath the mask of his gaiety and beautiful manners. There she found what she had most admired in Mangan, in Johnson, and in Browning: victory over self. "It was part of his perfect courage that he had learned small talk, banter, puns, games and dances; they were so many weapons to keep the blue devils at bay. He had to beguile the thing he was with perpetual cap and bells."[40] Before he became the distinguished public actor which his role required, he was not

merry. And he died well, with the same humility, manners, and kindness which had marked his reign. When he called his friend John Huddleston, the Benedictine, to his bedside to hear his confession, he apologized to the mourning attendants for being "so unconscionably long a-dying." He expired with the tragicomic touch that had shadowed his career by issuing his last executive order on behalf of his mistress: "Don't let poor Nelly starve."

### V  *Finale*

Although 1897 may have been Louise's annus mirabilis, the toll was heavy. The long hours maintained at Auburndale Post Office and the longer ones expended on grueling literary chores caused the inevitable physical collapse that occurred in the spring of that year. As she explained to Dr. Richard Garnett:

Last April I broke down under a sharp attack of meningitis (my first illness) due, as the Dr. and nurse insisted, against my opinion, to overwork, or rather, to prolonged lack of relaxation . . . . I still have to fight with insomnia, the most unheard-of dragon heretofore. So this fact influenced my mother, at least, in urging me to cut loose from my sentence of "four years hard"; not wholly expired. I am positive that U.S.P.O. and the discipline thereof, has improved my character: but I suspect that it has, with equal obviousness, ruined my intellect! I have not uttered a line of verse for just a year. I cannot, however, weep over the questionable calamity . . . .[41]

While Louise's account was not strictly accurate in describing this illness as her first (she had shown a tendency toward increasing deafness[42]), she was right about the resignation. She returned to the post office in late May after an absence of six weeks; but, early in July, she submitted her resignation. It was a day late, the fifth; but, from every other point of view, it was her celebration of Independence Day. On that very day she wrote to the Reverend William H. Van Allen: "'The snare is broken; and we are delivered!' I am so pleased, I cannot refrain from dancing: though dancing was never in my line. Which clearly proves that dancing is a motion born of the primitive instinct of human joy. Now for freedom, and the ultimate alms house! I am even as I was four years agone, only with the po'try carefully drained out, and some character, let us hope, screwed in."[43]

Naturally, her chief English correspondent got the news, if some-

what later in the month. She wrote to Herbert Clarke: "I'm a full-fledged ex-postmiss, thanks to 'whatever gods there be.' Not a plan of any sort in my head, yet . . . Luddy! If I bain't glad to stretch my legs, and be penniless and *free*, even for one summer."[44] That summer and the next were to be spent at Five Islands, Maine.

# Anticlimax

FIVE Islands, where Fred Holland Day also spent the summers, was really a promontory of the mainland stretching out into Casco Bay, a bit north of Portland. Perhaps, at this depressed state of Louise's fortunes, it reminded her too much of longed-for South Devon: "all steep cliffs facing seaward, of whitest granite, coves, beaches, pasture-lands, and great tidal rivers running inland, abreast, for perhaps twenty miles."[1] The natives were friendly ("incomparable," in Louise's words); but, with typical Yankee lack of subtlety, they inquired if her mother was likely to "marry again"; if she was "of age" herself;[2] if Fred Day, vacationer-neighbor and regular visitor, was her "feller."[3] Between swimming and sailing, Louise's nose took on the hue of martyrs' days' vestments; but, if more relaxed, her fingers kept the telltale mark of writer's ink while at the shore and, of course, in Auburndale where she returned for the winter.

Two projects preoccupied her: a translation of the *Fioretti* of St. Francis and the compilation *England and Yesterday*. A third work, also to appear before the end of 1898, was another translation, from the French of Louis Morvan's *The Secret of Fougereuse*. During the same period, she composed a long narrative poem, "The Martyrs' Idyl," published first by *Harper's* as a poem in its Christmas number of 1898 and, later, by Houghton Mifflin in book form as *The Martyrs' Idyl and Shorter Poems,* in 1899. In 1899, she also prepared the biographical sketch and notes for Professor Charles Swain Thomas' Riverside Literature Series edition of Matthew Arnold's *Sohrab and Rustum and Other Poems.* Meanwhile, Charles Dudley Warner had printed her old, but revised, article about John Keats in his edition of *A Library of the World's Best Literature Ancient and Modern.*[4]

Three facts emerge from Louise's productivity at this time: her growing concentration on the scholarly (editions and translations); her correspondingly increased concern with religious subjects and themes; and her waning hold upon poetic inspiration. Under-

standably, the experience of the preceding years had diminished her self-reliance and driven her to rely more on God. These developments, particularly the first two—scholarship and religion—became absorptions in the following years.

## I    *The Little Flowers of St. Francis*

Except for two chapters ("The Sermon to the Birds" and "The Wolf of Gubbio"), which were privately printed by Copeland and Day for Louise to distribute as Christmas gifts, her translation of the *Fioretti* was never printed. It was a loss to readers because there is no question that she was uniquely endowed by her own spirit to identify with the unworldliness of St. Francis and with his sense of the fraternal bond between man and nature. The merits of the little gift edition are unmistakable, but it is particularly regrettable that readers have no access to her rendering of St. Francis' "Hymn to the Sun" for which her sensitivity as a nature poet, as well as her intrinsically joyful spirit, had qualified her beyond a literal translator's merely professional competence.

As we have noted, Louise began the translation in the healing environment of Five Islands shortly after resigning from the onus of the post office; and, she recorded, "I am pegging at it daily; and, alas, in three weeks I have taken but one swim, and one spurt with the oars!"[5] Apparently, she persevered in her task; for she informed a friend in 1899 of both its completion and her reasons for restricting publication to the much-abridged Christmas gift edition: "I once did every word of the *Fioretti* into English, and have it somewhere near me in this huge desk, but I have never had it published, because a very good translation has come out, by Mr. T. W. Arnold; and besides that, there has also been issued a translation by Mr. Sebastian Evans of the "Speculum Perfectionis," a newly found manuscript of St. Francis' own time, which is a perfect mate for the *Fioretti* as we have it. So I contented myself with printing those two charming animal stories . . . ."[6]

## II    England and Yesterday

As a collection of poems, *England and Yesterday* lacks the substance of *A Roadside Harp* and *Happy Ending*. Along with *The Martyrs' Idyl and Shorter Poems*, it indicated the erosion of her

inspiration which she had apprehended would result from her government service. Although she worked on the collection while translating
the *Fioretti* at Five Islands, this compilation has little of the salti-
ness of Maine air and less of the breath of life. Most of its slim pages
are inflated, literally, with the inspirations of "Yesterday": the
"London" and "Oxford" sonnets, the "Two Irish Peasant Songs,"
"Athassel Abbey," and so on—all culled from *A Roadside Harp*—
and "Valediction: R. L. S., 1894" was reprinted from the "Postlude"
which had been appended to Alice Brown's *Stevenson.*

The title, derived from Stevenson, partly explains Louise's exces-
sive dependence upon old materials; for *England and Yesterday*
was intended for transatlantic readers who had not seen the previous
American publications. At the same time, Louise recognized, ruefully,
the paucity of new poems available for another publication to justify
her retirement and to boost her morale as a producing poet. Even
the publishing agreement with Grant Richards of London indicates a
desperation to get back into print at any cost: "Unless he sells over
250 copies, I'm to have no royalty at all; if he sells from 250 to 399, I
get a royalty from the 251st copy; . . . "[7] She was candid in admit-
ting to Dora Sigerson the compilation's dependence upon *A Roadside Harp,*[8] and she was franker still in calling her work "a sort
of ragged sheaf of lyrics."[9]

The handful of poems newly collected, however, disproves her
fear that her Muse was dead. Her tributes to Izaak Walton, Percy
Bysshe Shelley, and Emily Brontë assemble a verse pantheon of
literary "greats" that parallels the prose portraits collected earlier in
*A Little English Gallery.* In one memorable line she struck a
medallion image of Shelley as "That mounting, foolish, foam-bright
heart."[10] Emily Brontë, whose grave at Scarborough she had
once sought to memorialize suitably, received her epitaph in eight
lines:

> What sacramental hurt that brings
> The terror of the truth of things
> Had changed thee? Secret be it yet.
> 'Twas thine, upon a headland set,
> To view no isles of man's delight,
> With lyric foam in rainbow flight,
> But all a-swing, a-gleam, mid slow up-roar,
> Black sea, and curved uncouth sea-bitten shore.[11]

The Cavalier poems published in this collection are among her best in this Jacobite vein, and they are an appropriate sequel to the "Inquirendo" on Charles II in *Patrins:* "The Graham Tartan to a Graham," "A Footnote to a Famous Lyric" (Lovelace's "To Lucasta, On Going to the Wars"), and the oft-quoted "Writ in My Lord Clarendon his 'History of the Rebellion.'"

If the contents of *England and Yesterday* were meager, the dedications were multiplied according to the several divisions of the book. Publication involved a clan reunion under one cover: the "London Sonnets" to Herbert E. Clarke; the "Oxford" ones to Lionel Johnson; the "Lyrics" to Dora Sigerson and Clement Shorter; "Lines on Various Fly-Leaves" to Gwenllian Morgan; and an honorable mention to Alice Brown ("To A. B."), added to "Romans in Dorset." It was almost a valedictory party for the Muse, as if Louise sensed the drying up of the Pierian spring by doling out her slender harvest.

## III *Hack?*

Louise's last book in 1898 was a translation, *The Secret of Fougereuse*. Attracted by her verve among the medieval revivalists who had launched Cram's *Knight Errant* and her cultural leadership in the growing market of Catholic readers, Marlier and Callahan of Boston persuaded her to translate Louis Morvan's *Jehan de Fougereuse*. Translation was easy work for one with her facility in French, but she had sound misgivings about her talent for fiction: "I could as soon play the oboe as get a grasp on narrative."[12] However, the theme, as well as the fifteenth-century setting, appealed to her: religious vocation discovered through renunciation in the chivalrous times of "good King René" of the Book of Tournaments. Within the limitations of the original, her handling was competent. Her tone sensitively adhered to the antique motto on the title page: *"Tout passe fors aymer Dieu"* (Everything passes except love of God), which was to become the motif, if not the motto, of her own writing. The reviewers were generally kind, if not enthusiastic: *New Age* called it "pensive and tender"; *Bookman,* aptly, described it as "An old-fashioned but ever-delightful romance"; the *Daily News* complained that it was "exasperatingly obscure."[13]

Louise's only complaint was the injustice done to Morvan by featuring her name on the title page. She attempted to check the

error on the dedication page: "To Grace Denslow . . . the translator's share in this book." But, because her readers persisted in linking her with authorship, she explained: "The book is a 'skin-tight' translation from the French of M. Louis Morvan, of whom I never heard until Messrs. Marlier and Callahan asked me to turn him into American; and I fought long and hard to have his name on the title page. It seemed a point of honour to me, yet the publishers wished it simply 'from the French.' The result seems to be that nobody believes the story to be a translation . . . ."[14]

### IV   *Boston Public Library*

Neither *England and Yesterday* nor *The Secret of Fougereuse,* anymore than the privately circulated chapters of the *Fioretti,* sufficed to sustain the illusions of Five Islands or the short-lived independence that had made her want to dance on leaving the post office in Auburndale. She was still dependent, even precariously so. Her father's friends had been instrumental in effecting her former security; and now her own friends—Annie Fields, Thomas Wentworth Higginson, and Sarah Orne Jewett—rallied to her rescue. Miss Jewett, also an *habituée* of the Fields' circle, shared Louise's professional interests as writer, especially the common fund of Celtic lore which Miss Jewett had acquired during her residence in the Aran Isles. Previously, she had tried to get Louise an appointment in the Boston Public Library after the sorry affair of the Auburndale boycott; and she now pressed her objective with patience and persistence—efforts which finally culminated in Louise's appointment in January, 1899.[15]

However grateful she might have been, Guiney had not been eager, much less pushing; for she had received other encouragement that looked more tempting than return to the public treadmill. Two prospects glimmered enticingly: an invitation to join the *Atlantic's* "Men and Letters" department; an offer from Mark de Wolfe Howe[16] to write a life of Isaac Hecker for the Beacon Biography Series. But both offers presumed the nonextant in her case—sufficient private means to sustain her during periods of research and preparation. Reluctantly, she completed the standard application blank for employment in the Boston Public Library on Copley Square.

The application, still in the files of the Boston Public Library, made no mention of her long list of scholarly articles published, her twenty-odd books, or her administrative experience in the Auburndale Post Office. With something of classic understatement, she listed her qualifications as follows: "Know something of typewriting and a couple of foreign languages. Can read proof expertly. Have a fair knowledge of music (except orchestral scores),[17] and a slighter one of Gothic architecture. Have good general knowledge of English literature, especially that of the sixteenth and early seventeenth centuries, and of the history and archaeology of the same period."[18] Minutes of the trustees for December 9, 1898, authorized the library administration to employ Miss Guiney for special service (at fifty cents an hour) to index the Chamberlain Collection or to do similar work. The appointment was formally confirmed on January 22, 1899, for assignment to the Catalogue Room. A year and a half later, she was promoted to full-time basis at fifteen dollars a week.[19]

For almost two years she continued in the Catalogue Room where she occasionally checked Colonel Thomas Wentworth Higginson's Galatea Collection or the library's holdings in miracle plays or chartularies. Associates were congenial, especially the young poet, Philip Savage.[20] With Aunt Betty, Louise had moved into Boston to be close to her work, first to a "great town house" on Newbury Street and then to a small apartment on Pinckney Street.[21] From both she could walk easily to the library, often across the Public Gardens. Though the family had been reduced to taking in genteel boarders (such as Professor Bock of Boston University), life was regular and by no means unpleasant; and on weekends they enjoyed visits with Mrs. Guiney in Auburndale. Louise told Herbert Clarke that the library was "as beautiful a prison house as can be imagined .... Post office is a bad dream, to look back upon."[22] She was equally resigned, if not exactly sanguine, in reporting her fortunes to Dora Sigerson: "it is not tragic in the least, ... Besides, I like my daily chore."[23]

## V   The Martyrs' Idyl

In addition to the library's daily routine, she managed to continue her perennial ones. Hardly a month and a half after entering

the Catalogue Room, she was writing to Van Allen of two new literary projects, both obviously under way: "The Arnold begins and goes slowly, between huge interruptions. I have just scraped my verses together for another volume: H.M. & Co. I do not feel satisfied with it. It ought to be better than the *Harp,* but it isn't. 'Shades of the prison house' are over it and me. My breadwinning began in 1894, and my poetry ended, as of course I knew it would and must."[24]

The "Arnold," a biographical sketch and poem notes, was her share of C. S. Thomas' edition of *Sohrab and Rustum and Other Poems* for the Riverside Literature Series. Within the standard compact school text, she compressed the insights into Arnold which she had heretofore amplified in "Wilful Sadness in Literature." His "sweet reasonableness" and Classical austerity justified his acceptance as "a classic in his lifetime." His sustained crusade against smugness in society was all the rarer by virtue of a "lucid and urbane habit" generally wanting in reformers. Like Thoreau, she mistrusted that breed's tainted philanthropy, as well as fanatics of any ilk. Significantly, the little Arnold text went into three editions.

The other volume for "H.M. & Co." was also finished before her first year in the Library had expired: *The Martyrs' Idyl and Shorter Poems.*[25] Like those of *England and Yesterday,* its contents substantiated her grounds for the dissatisfaction confessed in the letter to Van Allen; for she had relied heavily upon old pieces scraped together. The thirty-page title poem itself had been printed a year earlier in *Harper's;* but many of the new lyrics included evidenced that her Muse was still fertile, if less frequently productive. Together with "The Martyrs' Idyl," these poems confirmed that the shades of the monastery, if not of the prisonhouse, were, indeed, beginning to enclose her. She immured herself in both antiquarian scholarship and in religion. "The Martyrs' Idyl" retells, in blank verse, the story of St. Didymus and Theodora during the persecution of Christians under Diocletian. As a narrative poem, it lacks the vigor which had distinguished "Tarpeia" in *The White Sail;* and, as drama, it compounds the ineptitude for dialogue which she had always freely acknowledged. The image of Cardinal Newman's *Callista* (only recently received as a gift from Herbert Clarke) overshadows a personal response to an incontrovertibly religious inspiration. The letter to Van Allen, her Episcopalian "confessor," reveals her misgivings during composition: her awareness of the in-

congruity of the simple *Acta Sanctorum* story with romantic love,
complicated further by imposition of formal Greek idyl to accommo-
date a late Alexandrian background where the subjects met martyrdom.[26]

But other poems in the same volume are convincing evidence of her
deepening spiritual commitment, as well as of her genuine contribu-
tion to religious expression of quality in the American lyric. These
poems confirm her renunciation of the world to gratify a profounder
hunger and also her entrance into expanding mystical experience.

### Sanctuary

High above hate I dwell:
O storms! farewell.
Though at my sill your daggered thunders play
Lawless and loud tomorrow as today,
To me they sound more small
Than a young fay's footfall:
Soft and far-sunken, forty fathoms low
In Long Ago,
And winnowed into silence on that wind
Which takes wars like a dust, and leaves but love behind.

Hither Felicity
Doth climb to me,
And bank me in with turf and marjoram
Such as bees lip, or the new-weaned lamb:
With golden barberry wreath,
And bluets thick beneath;
One grosbeak, too, mid apple-buds a guest
With bud-red breast,
Is singing, singing! All the hells that rage
Float less than April fog below our hermitage.[27]

### Deo Optimo Maximo

All else for use, One only for desire:
Thanksgiving for the good, but thirst for Thee:
Up from the best, whereof no man need tire,
Impel Thou me.

Delight is menace if Thou brood not by,
Power is a quicksand, Fame a gathering jeer.

Oft as the moon (though none of earth deny
These three are dear),

Wash me of them, that I may be renewed,
And wander free amid my freeborn joys:
Oh, close my hand upon Beatitude!
Not on her toys.[28]

Borderlands

Through all the evening,
All the virginal long evening,
Down the blossomed aisle of April it is dread
   to walk alone;
For there the intangible is nigh, the lost is ever-during;
And who would suffer again beneath a too-divine alluring,
Keen as the ancient drift of sleep on dying faces
   blown?

Yet in the valley,
At a turn of the orchard alley,
When a wild aroma touched me in the moist
   and moveless air,
Like breath indeed from out Thee, or as airy vesture round Thee,
Then was it I went faintly, for fear I had nearly found Thee,
O Hidden, O Perfect, O Desired! O first
   and final Fair![29]

These poems do not match Emily Dickinson's lightning flashes of
spiritual insight such as "Eternity shall be velocity or pause/
Precisely as the candidate preliminary was." They are as conventional
in form as the subscription of an outsider-immigrant seeking place
in a Brahmin world of letters would dictate; and the slightly relieved
conventionality is compounded by the rigidity of Catholic devotional
poetry comprehensible to dependent, untutored masses who strove
for a vision beyond their reach "in durance vile." They would, at
least, fan the fervor of hungry hearts disillusioned by their lot and
longing for dimensions demanded by their unfulfilled capacities.
Besides what they revealed of Louise's personal disappointments
or her reiteration of doctrines proclaimed as universal, they opened
a mystical vista which was penetrated, if not fathomed. Unlike Emily
Dickinson, whom an atrophied Calvinism still supported securely,

Louise could not go the whole distance of subjective experience because of the heavy burden of her traditional erudition and "feudal" obligation to her Catholic constituency. But these poems touchingly evidence her retreat from the transience of activism to a more enduring reality.

## VI    *To England*

Nevertheless, Louise did not neglect responsible involvement in this world. Van Wyck Brooks, for example, lists her among the outspoken anti-imperialists opposing the Spanish-American War and the extension of Manifest Destiny into the Pacific.[30] Nor were the "goods" of this world wholly rejected during this period, and one in particular she clapped to her heart and treasured after discovering it by accident while browsing at Goodspeed's bookstalls, a rare copy of her beloved Vaughan's *Thalia Rediviva,* the fourth known to exist. It had survived by being bound inside a copy of his less valued *Olor Iscanus.*[31] The "find" thrilled her, but it also revived memories of the vow made with Gwenllian Morgan to complete the project hopefully launched in 1895.

Louise was soon chafing at the bonds of the "beautiful prison house" and longing again for England. Grade *B* Cataloguer Guiney, preferred to be a Grade *A* editor of seventeenth-century poets, as she made plain in a letter to Dora Sigerson:

Alas, my Muse is an absentee landlady! I am kept so busy, these latter years, on mere day-labouring, that I can write nothing, nor live for a day in my own tents. Perhaps I ought not to say "busy," though I am surely occupied enough; but I lack the mood .... Nevertheless, I have my snug dream of a long life, say in Red Lion Square ... where I shall always have a raven to bring muffins for the family, (and celery, and clothes, and pin-money,) and where I shall have nothing on earth to do but to dig in the seventeenth century, and edit and edit, and live in the odour of folios .... It would be "Paradise enow," I warrant.[32]

The dream persisted, for she wrote to Dora that autumn: "Some day, when I am free (i.e., moth-eaten and tame with years) I am going to emigrate to some hamlet that smells strong of the Middle Ages, and put cotton-wool in my ears, and swing out clear from this very smart century altogether."[33] That Louise had already begun to plan this move she did not disclose; but she had privately con-

tacted Edward Henry Clement, editor of the *Transcript,* months
earlier in a vain attempt to get him to underwrite her English residence
as an overseas correspondent.[34] By May, 1900, she was willing to
risk all uncertainties in order to take the step for "Liberty and Lit-
teryture, yea, and for Fleet Street, E.C." She so informed the
cautioning Clarke: "No, Sir, I have no sort of pot-boiler in mind,
whereby I shall continue to live in Lunnon after I get there, presumably
in the character of a stowaway; but I'll quote you one Montrose
about fearing one's fate too much. Wait until next year! for explode
I must not until then."[35]

She submitted her resignation to the trustees of the Boston Public
Library on December 27, 1900. By February, 1901, accompanied by
Aunt Elizabeth Doyle, she was in England once more. The crossing
was not a luxury cruise; for the  cattle boat *Devonian,* carried
seven hundred bullocks and only three other passengers besides the
aunt and niece. But the pair rejoiced at the familiar look of Dartmouth
in Devon: "exactly similar to our Five Islands," she wrote back
to her former library colleagues.[36] Moreover, Dartmouth was cheaper
than London through which they had passed quickly; and, it
smelled of the Middle Ages!

CHAPTER 10

# The Old Home

LOUISE'S residence in England was to be permanent and her residences there many. Except for two crossings to Boston (a visit of six weeks in 1906; and a longer stay in 1909–10 to attend her dying mother), she was an expatriate in all save citizenship and patriotism. In December, 1902, her aunt died in Oxford;[1] and her mother (who had visited them twice in England) returned to America permanently in 1904. Most of her English years were spent close to Oxford, but she occasionally spent her winters on the Cornwall or Devon coast where living was warmer and less expensive. Twice she crossed to the Continent: once to Bruges to try to arrange schooling for her young cousin, Ruth Guiney;[2] once to visit her old friend Grace Denslow, now married and living at Evian-les-Bains. In May, 1902, Louise gave in Ireland her lecture "Raleigh and Spenser in Munster" before the National Literary Society in Dublin. But extended absence from Oxford and its Bodleian Library was rare.

During 1912–16, Louise became practically identified with "Longwall Cottage," Oxford; and it became distinguished by the Stars and Stripes that hung from her windows during World War I. There three orphaned Guineys joined her to swell her ménage and to multiply her responsibilities: her young cousins, Grace and Ruth, and their little niece, Mary Louise Martin. As the hardships of the war increased, she found it necessary to seek more modest lodgings in Gloucestershire, where she was somewhat removed from the beloved Bodleian but amid her favorite Cotswolds. From 1917 throughout 1918, illness, which curtailed her scholarly preoccupations, aggravated her proneness to deafness and enforced long periods of rest.

Notwithstanding the discouragement of these years which were pinched by want and inconvenienced by frequent moves, her industry was unflagging and her talent far from atrophied. If hardly staggering by Scott's or Balzac's output; the list of her books published during this period would vindicate the careers of most profes-

sionals. Besides *The Mount of Olives and Primitive Holiness* (1902), these included *Katherine Philips, "The Matchless Orinda," Robert Emmet,* and *Hurrell Froude, Memoranda and Comments*—all published in 1904; *Thomas Stanley, His Original Lyrics* (1907); *Blessed Edmund Campion* (1908); *Happy Ending* (1909); *Post-Liminium: Essays and Critical Papers by Lionel Johnson* (1911)[4]; *Some Poems of Lionel Johnson, Newly Selected* (1912); and the posthumously published *Recusant Poets* (1938), the second volume of which still remains unedited.[5]

Louise's verses during the same span, though diminished by her concentration on scholarship and editing, are still impressive in number and quality, if insufficient in quantity to warrant a new collection after the posthumous, revised edition of *Happy Ending* in 1927: "The Poplar" (*Harper's Monthly,* June, 1903); "St. Francis Endeth His Sermon" (*Century,* August, 1904); "Colloquy" (*McClure's,* January, 1906); "Astraea" (*Harper's Monthly,* March, 1906); "Pascal" (*Century, July, 1907); "Beati Mortui" (Atlantic,* January, 1908); "A Carol of Beasts" (*McClure's,* December, 1908); "The Kings" (*Current Literature,* June, 1910); "Davy" (*Century,* November, 1912); "To a Motor" (*Atlantic,* April, 1913); and "Lyric Miracle" and "Speed," both printed in the September, 1915, issue of *Nation.* Besides these, there were many others which often appeared in the always hospitable *Catholic World* and in *McClure's* where Willa Cather accorded Louise's submissions a special welcome.[6]

The articles written during Louise's English years have a focal sharpness and relevance wanting even in the best of those in *Patrins.* In a sense, they were her bread and butter; and they showed a late-learned adaptation to the advice of Ferris Greenslet about the changing nature of the mass market.[7] *The Nation, The Tablet, Month, The Catholic World, Notes and Queries, The Dublin Review* and *Ave Maria* became her principal outlets. If she made a greater concession than had been her wont to the current topic and the average reader, it was insufficient to label her a working journalist. The scholarly subject was still uppermost, and the appeal was increasingly toward Catholic concern. But even while she continued to be fascinated with obscure figures of the seventeenth century like William Cartwright and Digby Dolben,[8] she kept her mind open to the new. She became, for example, one of the early promoters

of Gerard Manley Hopkins.[9] As always, tradition and progress remained the twin poles of her world outlook.

## I  *The Seventeenth Century*

On disembarking from the *Devonian* in 1901, Louise had gone straight to London; for she was eager to plunge into the literary current. London proved less hospitable to her fortunes than to fabled Dick Whittington's, for publishers were either "out" to the stranger from America or not to her liking. Because the yellowed manuscript of her Delavigne translation proved unmarketable,[10] Louise, in desperation, as Aunt Betty began to fail, read proofs for a New York publisher—hardly an improvement over the Catalogue Room of the Boston Public Library. But the velvety moss of England was under her foot, and the seventeenth century was always at hand in Oxford or in Wales—the dream that had beckoned her— and her editing mission increasingly absorbed her between 1902 and 1907: first Vaughan, to complete the cherished project now that she was close to her Welsh collaborator, Gwenllian Morgan; then on to "The Matchless Orinda" and Thomas Stanley, of forgotten merit; and, if possible, to that whirling dervish of the era's religious confusion, William Alabaster.

By 1902 Louise had edited and published in a single volume Vaughan's *Mount of Olives* with its companion piece, *Primitive Holiness,* "as set forth in the life of Paulinus, Bishop of Nola." Both prose works had been faithfully, even lovingly, edited; but prospects for the "big" Vaughan volume, for which Guiney and Morgan had been collecting notes for years, had been already dimmed when the Muses Library *Vaughan* by E. K. Chambers had appeared in print late in 1896. Louise, whose judgment was always fair even in reversals, had continued to persevere in her project because she honestly thought that the Muses Library text was "bad-bad"[11] and because Israel Gollancz had encouraged Miss Guiney and Miss Morgan to edit Vaughan's *Silex Scintillans* for the Temple Classics.[12] In Gollancz's absence printers so bungled the edition that the two ladies refused to accept it as their work. When Professor George E. B. Saintsbury's definitive edition of minor Carolian poets was announced in 1903, Louise conceded defeat and, like the gallant Cavaliers whom she often celebrated, she drank Saintsbury's health

but without the usual Jacobite rider: "And send this Crum—well down."[13] Years later when Dr. F. E. Hutchinson asserted undisputed claim to Vaughan studies by his authoritative *Henry Vaughan: A Life and Interpretation* (Oxford, 1947), some still respectfully remembered Guiney and Morgan for their scholarly pioneering in Vaughan's valley of the Usk. In grateful retrospect, Charles Morgan wrote of them in the *Sunday Times:*

The book's origin is, in a sense, romantic, for it is the fulfillment of a purpose to which two ladies devoted a great part of their lives . . . .

It may be hazarded that the two ladies might have allowed themselves more imaginative license than Dr. Hutchinson, a strict historian, has been willing to take, and I, for one, would not have rebuked them.[14]

In *Katherine Philips,* the title personage, who was known to her little circle as "Orinda," was Vaughan's neighbor and partisan to Cavaliers and Royalists in rejection of the Establishment for Church and King. Yet this did not tempt Louise to bias or mar her evaluation. She was familiar with Edmund Gosse's chapter on "The Matchless Orinda" in his *Seventeenth Century Studies* (1883), but she preferred to go back to Sir Charles Cotterell's 1668 folio of the Philips poems for her own scrupulously annotated selections. She conceded that "the matchless" one's verses "have less magic" than one expected in a Royalist singer; for they veered "into the explicities which are the borderlands of prose." Orinda's contractions were "rough"; and the chorus of praise which hailed ("and never spoiled her") in her day was "a tribute to character rather than to genius." Nevertheless, Louise—faithful to her belief in the great meaning in minor things—maintained that "no one who would study the history of English intellectual development on the distaff side . . . , will forbear some measure of acquaintance with 'Orinda,' queen of those virtuous poets who were among the public successes of the not-yet-understood Restoration."[15] "Orinda," more than an apologist for the Puritan-maligned Restoration, was a cultivated woman whose talent for appreciation and whose personal charm in stimulating better writers than she herself was, had made her the leader of a sparkling circle long before aristocratic French ladies opened their salons in the eighteenth century and longer still before women received a feeble political franchise in England and America in the twentieth century. Louise's critique of Katherine Philips as a

poet (the Restoration's Anne Bradstreet) focused on Orinda's faculty for appreciating and for patronizing the talent of others— a rare talent in any age and one which George Harvey Genzmer, in the *Dictionary of National Biography,* later ascribed to Louise herself: "opulent in sympathy."[16] But Genzmer had also credited Louise with "precision" in scholarship, if essentially intuitive and impressionistic. Though Louise could not justly extend the latter compliment to "Orinda," she acknowledged that Katherine Philips, if only a minor writer, had by her educated inferences and sympathetic intuitions avoided the pedantry befogging so much modern scholarship.

In the same year that Louise published *Thomas Stanley* (1907), the first complete printing of Stanley's original lyrics, she had observed in her article on "Literary Spying" that "sympathy, if only abstinent and incurious, is knowledge."[17] The exactions of editing may have forfeited some of the opulence of the amateur critic of *A Little English Gallery* to the professionalism of the seasoned editor of Stanley's poems, but the resultant precision did not lack sympathy. She had to collect many variants to resolve her selections; and she sifted them carefully for her finished text. Yet the personality of the author, who had composed his songs in the cross fire of Cavalier and Roundhead, shone undiminished. A far better poet than "Orinda," Stanley matched her in being "free of stain" in a society attuned to the amatory. Like her, he cultivated his own garden:

Through the Civil Struggle, the Commonwealth, the Restoration, he had followed a way of peace, without blame, and he is almost the only poet of the stormy time who is absolutely unaffected by it. He at least, need not be discounted as a pathetic broken crystal: he can be judged on his own little plot of ground, without allowances, and by our strictest modern standards. His bright best, his *viridaria,* have borne victoriously the lava-drift of nearly three centuries. An amorist of even temper and malice prepense, a railer with a sound heart, an untyrannic master of his Muse, Stanley sings low to his small jocund lyre, and need not be too curiously questioned about his sincerity. How can it matter? He gives delight; he deserves the bays.[18]

The book about William Alabaster, which would have rounded out her studies of seventeenth-century poets in 1902–7, never materialized; but its title was actually announced as "A Forgotten Poet, William Alabaster: His Life and Works, 1567–1640." Bertram

Dobell, who had begun amassing material on Alabaster after discovering a manuscript of his poems, generously shared his finds
with Guiney for her projected treatment. Louise acknowledged that
the manuscript made her opinion of Alabaster go "up and up":
"really a score of splendid sonnets . . . to go into an English treasury,"
deserving "a more learned editor."[19] But she returned "the
precious lendings" to Dobell in August, 1904; and she wrote nothing
on Alabaster until she included him among *Recusant Poets* years
later. He had interested her particularly as a weather vane of his
troubled times; for he had been spun about by the doctrinal winds
to which Ben Jonson and John Donne, and so many others, had
responded: Catholic at several periods of his life and, during one of
these, a Jesuit in Rome; and, finally, a confirmed Anglican Preb-
endary of St. Paul's.[20] But Louise feared that he had "drowned
his beautiful poetic gift in running after cabalistic philosophy."[21]

## II   *Recall to Reality*

Although Louise never relinquished her zeal for "grubbing for
facts,"[22] she emerged in the spring of 1906 from her shaft into the
lodes of the seventeenth century to sniff the salubrious air of Evian-
les-Bains, a fashionable spa in France. Grace Denslow, now married
to a Swiss (M. Émil Favre), had invited her to take a holiday with
them. The brief reunion was pleasant, although Louise returned
"quite as fagged" as she had gone. But, hardly returned to Oxford,
she received a cable that her mother was gravely ill; and, within a
fortnight, she had returned to Boston to her ailing parent's side as
"a goodish sort of nurse, and very glad to be here."[23] When Mrs.
Guiney had recovered sufficiently, Louise took her to Plymouth on
Massachusetts Bay, where they were house guests of her close friend
and benefactor,[24] Miss Anne Whitney, the sculptress who had
executed the Keats bust for the Hampstead Memorial. Satisfied that her mother was progressing under the care of a good doctor
and a reliable nurse, Louise returned to Oxford before the opening
of the Michelmas term.
During her relatively short stay, she was undoubtedly questioned
persistently about her preference for living in England. Her best
response, which followed closely upon her return to Oxford, was
published in the *Atlantic* (April, 1907): "On a Preference for Living

in England." *Scribner's Magazine* had previously published her account of "English Reserve" while she was still in Boston tending her mother; and "English Weather," also appeared in it in November, 1907. A more specialized apologia appeared in *Ave Maria* (February, 6, 1909) under the title "Catholicism in England: A Non-Scientific Survey," in which she contrasted English and American Catholics. Plainly, she felt an obligation to explain herself—as well as Americans and Englishmen to each other.

### III  *England versus America*

In her lesser sphere, Louise was doing what Irving and Longfellow (and Hawthorne and James) had done to build bridges between Old and New Worlds. She began "On a Preference for Living in England" by acknowledging that her paper intended a brief less for those who go than for those who cannot stay: "European passports must be cheerfully furnished to our artistic fraternity." In the spirit of Hawthorne and James, she conceded that "Whoever has a rage for origin, a lust for things at first-hand, is foredoomed to chafe at a civilization which dates from this morning, and spends its energies on tasks far other than the effort to see life steadily and see it whole." In Guiney's view, "There is something rational, surely, in an attraction which has already drained the United States of so much genius, literary and artistic; which has resulted in forming so many wise, devoted, and detached critics to whip us up to our ideals, and remind us of our sins."[25]

Yet her kinship with "Our Old Home" went deeper than Hawthorne's ancestor hunting and James's esthetic archaeology. Her profoundly Catholic humanism had made her, in her own words, "organically European" from childhood. She had been so spiritually rooted in the Old World that she had always risked losing touch with, as well as her sympathy for, the pace of change in a New England no longer pastoral. She chafed at *"Hustlerium Tremens sive Americanitis"*:[26] its "epic newness," its "startling developments," its "too-eager gynaecocracy."[27] In contrast, she wrote,

You know [in England] that you will never long to get anywhere in particular, or strain after anything except salvation .... Time and Eternity are pretty nearly one in the moist amethyst-colored air. You realize fully that

the ozone is gone out of it, and that the sad heart of the earth beneath has bled for long. But you also realize that you are acquiring from contact with these an almost sportive sense of the unseen and the supernatural, and a sense which unravels essence from accident, true from plausible, lasting from uncertain, innocent from profane . . . . Not that our happier natures in the United States have not at all times attained to them. But their exemption from the hurly-burly is a bought one; you do not have to buy it in England. It commends itself to the indigent, for it is a flowing fountain in the streets.[28]

Henry James could have understood her sense of the past, and Hawthorne would have appreciated her opinions of popularly vaunted American individualism and alleged Old World conformism. For she felt that democratic leveling at home enforced a deadly mediocrity at the expense of freedom; but that England, despite its structured social hierarchy, sustained the individualism of privacy at all levels. The English, at least, could indulge a passion for silence or seclusion without either general indictment or private guilt complex: "[One] will not be asked by an interviewer at 4 a.m., and at the point of a moral bayonet, for his impressions concerning problems fiscal or forensic. If he is understood to have exhibited in the Salon, or to have published a sonnet, not a living British creature will think any the better of him for it."[29] Without arousing suspicion of treasonable eccentricity, any Englishman could be publicly tired of keeping awake, toeing the mark, affecting interest, or even wearing an intelligent expression. In America, on the other hand, civic orthodoxy obliged one to be tortured slowly on the public scaffold and to smile inanely until the hangman's noose snapped fatally at the term of a long-drawn out martyrdom.

Yet Louise was no Anglophile, much less an Anglo-maniac, for she defended loyally and gratefully the virtues of America. The lady laureate of Civil War minstrelsy, and the erstwhile tourist who had thrilled to the sight of Old Glory flying "In the Docks," had not shifted allegiance. Her customary gift to foreign friends was a little package neatly enveloping a folded Stars and Stripes. She flew her own "huge old Auburndale" one over Longwall Cottage throughout the Great War. When Grace and Ruth Guiney joined her at Oxford, Louise proudly reported that they were "Catholicizing at a great rate"; but she noted, in the same letter, that "de-Americanizing" was her least wish.[30] When Katherine Tynan Hinkson, the poetess,

made the mistake of calling Louise an "Irish-American," she instantly repudiated the hyphenation: "plain 'American' is my due and suits me well."[31] Any animus which she showed toward Woodrow Wilson and America's delayed entrance into World War I derived less from commitment to England (though, understandably, she deprecated bombs over old Bodley) than from chagrin at America's reluctance to accept the destiny of world leadership. To her last days, she cherished the American's achievement and potential: "He has wrought for himself the white ideal of government; he belongs to a growing, not a decaying society." But he needed also to hear "our sunken footfalls ages before we were born" and the love that called to him "from towers a great way off."[32]

## IV  *De Profundis*

But England was not Eden. In 1907, the Bodleian archives were even more subterranean than the Catalogue Room of the Boston Public Library. The seventeenth-century authors on whom she had labored were golden, but they yielded no gold. Clement Shorter, now married to Dora Sigerson, had used his influence to obtain an invitation from Dr. Robertson Nicoll, editor of the English Men of Letters Series, for Louise to write a biography of William Hazlitt. But, at this depressed state of her affairs, "Hazlitt's child" confessed her inability to accept, and did so in a rare jeremiad; for Augustine Birrell's study had usurped the field, and Louise was discouraged:

It is simply impossible. Whatever fire was originally in me has died out for lack of a flue; I am, I will say, not embittered . . . but atrophied. If I ever finish long-begun and long-interrupted tasks like the Vaughan, Alabaster, St. Frideswide,[33] etc. I shall do almost more than now I hope for; but I shall never be able to plan and carry out with my old zest. You don't know what it is to have to live on public praise; to have done your very best in composing or editing some sixteen books, and to draw from them in the lump . . . not three guineas a year, seldom as much as forty-five shillings! . . . And therefore, knowing that, though I keep up a brisk step, and a grin, I have no least heart to undertake Hazlitt, or anything else which is a fresh enterprise.[34]

On the last day of 1908, she was summoned to Boston where her mother's condition had worsened; and her stay lasted more than a year. On arriving in Boston Harbor, she had gone suddenly deaf.[35]

Other cares multiplied. Their Auburndale home had to be sold "at a slaughtering price."[36] Mrs. Guiney had to be brought into Boston to share an apartment with Louise, again on Pinckney Street. When not tending her, Louise wrote at the nearby Athenaeum, collecting her poems for an obvious valediction, *Happy Ending.*[37] When Houghton Mifflin published the book in December, 1909, it was dedicated to Anne Whitney. As the New Year began, Louise, who collapsed from exhaustion, required care first at the Fields' and then at St. Elizabeth's Hospital. When Mrs. Guiney died suddenly on February 5, 1910, Louise, worn by fatigue and racked by anxiety, fell seriously ill. After six weeks of care and convalescence at the Newton home of her friend, Dr. Alice M. Jackman, she felt impelled to sail for England. Her distress, and desperation, is evident in her hasty note to Fred Holland Day: "Sonny, WHEN can I see you? . . . I'm just about distracted and must flee (Leyland Line) and may the Lord have mercy on my soul! because I have no idea how I can ever manage all the unsettled affairs between!"[38]

She left Boston in May, 1910, never to return; for England had become her refuge. Shortly after landing, she wrote Bertram Dobell from Derbyshire that she was back on the trail of "friend Alabaster."[39] If not gold, the graves of the seventeenth century promised the peace of oblivion.

# The Catacombs

THE catacombs enclosing burrowing Louise Guiney were not only the labyrinthine ways of seventeenth-century archives. The vaults of the Old Faith, into which the citadel-church of the late nineteenth and early twentieth centuries had withdrawn defensively, beckoned deeper. There she retreated, finding solace, along with immurement from a turbulent mainstream, as her direction had consistently pointed there. Her choice had been elected, but she thereby had cut herself off from contemporary sympathy. Her writing had always been religious in tone, infused with a Christian humanism; and, after her departure for England in 1901, it had become increasingly Catholic in focus as was apparent in her handling of Royalist-Cavalier poets. John Donne, for example, was "A Lost Catholic Poet":[1] and the Restoration had revived Catholic culture, but only secretly had it edged toward reunion with Rome.

Even Emmet, the ill-starred Irish patriot, exercised more than the appeal of doomed youth and Hibernian hopes. His execution in 1804 had undermined any bridge of reconciliation between Old and New Orders. Like most advocates of Irish nationalism, he had been Protestant. His execution for "treason" was only an episode, historically, in the evolution of Irish independence culminating in 1922. But, because he had seemed a symbol of the burial of ancient divisions, she had rushed her biography of 1904 into publication to coincide with the hundredth anniversary of his death.[2]

Although the work manifested her persistent fascination with young and brilliant failures, it also demonstrated that, proximity to Ireland notwithstanding, she was still unseduced by the myth of the Irish Question. Actually, she anticipated James Joyce's indictment of Ireland as "the old sow that eats her farrow."[3] She conceded that the story of starry-eyed Emmet reflected "a great unwritten chapter of perfidy behind his lonely ineffectual blow struck for national freedom."[4] She frankly acknowledged the irony of Protestant leadership and the fickleness of the Catholic rabble in Emmet's futile seizure of Dublin Castle. He was less Irish and less denomina-

tional than universal as a hero: "To be unbiased and Irish is to love Robert Emmet; to be generously English is to love him; to be American is to love him anyhow."[5]

Her interpretation was not surprising. She had consistently rejected the role of Hiberian or Catholic polemicist. But, in the love story of Emmet and his sweetheart, Sarah Curran, which was resolved after his death by Sarah's marriage to the English Captain Sturgeon who served with Wellington at Waterloo, Louise envisioned the burial of ancient animus.

### I  *Oxford Movement*

Louise's release in the same year of *Hurrell Froude: Memoranda and Comments* reflects her active participation in a genuine Oxford Movement of which the pseudo-medievalism of the *Knight Errant* and the "arty" catholicities of Cram's "Order of the White Rose" were juvenile transatlantic parodies. Louise was not up to gamesmanship when the spiritual stakes were so high, and her membership in the Romanist community of Oxford and England was confirmation, not baptism. The members of the group were fascinatingly alive and, intellectually, astounding. They enjoyed hiking with each other to shrines, such as St. Frideswide's, on feast days; and they laughingly called themselves "the Peripatetic Papists." They had their own intelligentsia peerage, who assembled in Louise's Oxford rooms: the Meynells, Father Joseph Rickaby, Monsignor Robert Hugh Benson, Prior Vincent McNabb, and Dom Bede Camm.

Until residence in England, Louise had known few Catholics of this elite. Characteristically, she launched a Newman crusade to restore the cardinal's rooms at Littlemore. She hounded Wilfrid Meynell and the *Tablet* into supporting the cause—and won, if posthumously; for the ceremony dedicating Newman's memorial on April 2, 1964, acknowledged Louise's role by a photostatic copy of her pleading letter to Meynell of March 18, 1902.[6] In the exhumation of one reputation, she unearthed another neglected one, far more to her fancy: Hurrell Froude, the forgotten inspiration of Newman and of the original Oxford Movement. For Froude was a fighter who had died at thirty-two.

On her personal annotated copy of *Hurrell Froude: Memoranda and Comments,* Louise had linked in an epigraph from Isaias: "He

has made me a chosen arrow."[7] Froude had all the ingredients of
the Guiney hero formula—youth, idealism, pugnacity, and early
death. That he had lived so briefly or accomplished so little visibly
only confirmed her summation of M. Henri's *raison d'être*: "Vital
and unexhausted spirits, under no subjection to results, can afford ...
to die anonymous .... He was a mere man of genius."[8] Yet, if
Froude, the fighting Anglican, had little lasting influence ascribable
to his works, he was "the lost Pleiad of the Oxford Movement."[9]
She quoted Principal Fairbairn's epigram: "Hurrell Froude lives
in Newman."[10] She concluded that Froude, a close companion
of Newman at Oxford, had given the cardinal "every single one
of his theories."[11]

Publication of *Hurrell Froude* had been attended by disappointments. Longmans had contracted for and then rejected it. The
division of contents, understandably, had jeopardized acceptance;
for the presentation of material was almost as modern as today's
cinema with its interweaving of multiple viewpoints. The long
preface was her own, and the "Comments" refracted the opinions of
Froude's contemporaries. Together, they challenged the reader to
form his own estimate of a phenomenon as complex as *Rashomon,*
through "the unfolding of a soul."[12]

## II  *The Jesuits*

If *Hurrell Froude* was Anglo-Catholic, *Blessed Edmund Campion* (New York, 1908) was Roman Catholic, *à l'outrance.* Louise's
association with Jesuits was old and dear; for, as a child, she had
been a member of the Immaculate Conception Parish on Boston's
Harrison Avenue, which had been founded and was conducted by
Jesuit fathers. The Jesuits had taught her own father at Holy Cross
College, and to its library she had committed all her father's books
before leaving for England. The priest most frequently entertained
in her home in America had been the Reverend Thomas Gasson of
Boston College. When Louise Chandler Moulton expressed a
tentative interest in the church, Louise could recommend only the
Jesuits Gasson and Rockwell "who would come up to your idea
or mine."[13] At the university, where she was rapidly becoming an
Oxford anchoress, the Reverend Arthur F. Day, S.J., the Catholic
Rector, was one of her closest friends. Her deep admiration of him

inspired her verse tribute, "To One Who Would Not Spare Himself"—"A censer playing from a heart all fire . . . ."[14]

Increasingly, Louise's correspondents came to number Jesuits: the Reverends Thomas Shandelle, Michael Earls, James J. Daly, and Geoffrey Bliss. The attachment was natural: the Society had been founded by the soldier-saint, Ignatius of Loyola, and its motto, "A.M.D.G.," was one she lived by, militantly: "For the Greater Glory of God."[15] Nevertheless, her admiration of Jesuits forfeited no inner self-direction, as she informed her Episcopalian friend, Father Van Allen: "I will say quite frankly that while I have great affection for the Jesuits . . . , I do not especially admire their system, either educational or moral . . . ." But Edmund Campion, the Oxford luminary and Tudor martyr (canonized on October 25, 1970, by Pope Paul VI), was hardly a subject likely to miss her treatment.[16]

Louise's biography of the heroic proctor of St. John's College was published in 1908, both in London and New York; and it was dedicated to "Campion's Brothers of the English Province of the Society of Jesus."[17] With *Patrins* and *Happy Ending,* it was one of only three of her books to go into a second edition (1914).[18] For the facts of Campion's story, her work leaned heavily on earlier studies by Robert Parsons, William Allen, Richard Simpson, and John Pollen. It successfully avoided the inherent melodrama of Campion's career, exploited by Robert Hugh Benson in *Come Rack, Come Rope.* By focusing on the perplexing confusions of religious loyalties in Elizabethan England, she eliminated incredible villains and instant-infallible heroes. Even Campion, the steadfast recusant who endured the hanging, drawing, and quartering at Tyburn, gains credibility by an earlier temporizing; for the doubts of his Oxford days become in the book a heavier interior cross than the barbarous public torture of the last hours. He emerges as a gentle but brilliant humanist and a promising successor to scholarly John Colet and William Grocyn, whom ironic circumstance propelled more brutally toward the fate of Thomas More. Such humanization enabled Guiney to transcend her usual difficulties with narrative, and she added a tragic note not often associated with martyrdom. For the irresistible eloquence which had skyrocketed his early career to acclaim and office trapped him at Lyford Grange when his pursuers were closing in on the secret

mass-house. He had yielded, fatally, to the entreaties of the recusant congregation for one last sermon.

His eloquence never deserted him subsequently, whether on the rack in the Tower of London, in private interrogation with Elizabeth and Leicester, or on trial, after torture, in Westminster Hall. Campion's was an authentic Renaissance style, one radiating the vision which George Chapman's vigorous translation of Homer had imparted to the young Keats. In Louise's own sensitive response to the felicity of Campion's language, she anticipated by forty years Evelyn Waugh's praise of the style that distinguished Campion's early *History of Ireland*.[19] Though the *History* is hardly more than a brochure, "the melodious phrases fall into place" effortlessly, thereby convincing the reader that Lord Burghley and Sir Francis Walsingham killed a book, as well as a man, when they sent Campion to Tyburn.[20] For just as Father Robert Parsons, Campion's Jesuit partner in the covert English mission, had confirmed the recusant John Shakespeare in the Old Faith, Campion himself had supplied, through Holinshed's edition of *History of Ireland,* the dramatic description of Wolsey's fall which son William, almost verbatim, incorporated into the second scene of Act IV of *Henry VIII.*

Campion kept his eloquence to the end. Like More at the block confessing himself "the King's good servant" (if God's, first), Campion's last words to the mob, before the hurdle was pulled from under him, invoked a blessing on the Elizabeth who might have saved him (and, privately, wished to): "to your Queen and my Queen, unto whom I wish a long, quiet reign, with all prosperity."[21]

No remote mystic was Edmund Campion, but a man of his age, with much endearing circumstance about and in him . . . . But in his kinship with his place and time, his peculiar greatness, his scholarship lightly worn, . . . he was a great Elizabethan too. He had sacrificed his fame and changed his career. He had spent himself for a cause the world can never love, and by doing so he has courted the ill-will of what passed for history, up to our day. But no serious student now mistakes the reason why his own England found no use for her "diamond" other than the strange use to which she put him. He is sure at last of justice . . . [22]

### III   *English versus American Catholics*

As Louise's visit to Boston in 1906 had involved her in an apologia for her preference for living in England, her expanded circle of

Catholic friends at Oxford led her to make comparisons between English and American Catholics. She had counted relatively few Catholics at home in the close circle of her friends. Her earliest intimate had been Rachel Norton, a Jewess; Fred Holland Day was, vaguely, Unitarian; Ralph Adams Cram, militantly High Church; Alice Brown, a "pantheist"; and the Reverend William H. Van Allen (always "Father" to her) was the controversial Episcopalian Rector of Boston's Church of the Advent. Annie Fields, Sarah Orne Jewett, Louise Chandler Moulton, and Bliss Carman were all Protestants of various denominations. The Frohocks, who faithfully supervised her American business interests, were Swedenborgians.

The English Catholics increasingly in her company edified her by their zeal and intelligence; and she attempted, accordingly, to explain them to their American co-religionists because she wanted to share what she had found admirable in English Catholicism. Her first attempt was rejected by the Reverend Herman J. Heuser, editor of *The American Ecclesiastical Review,* on the venerable principle that all comparisons are odious and that this particular one was bound to rub American Catholic sensibilites the wrong way.[23] A more daring American editor, the Reverend Daniel E. Hudson, C.S.C., accepted it for *Ave Maria,* but with some revisions, as "Catholicism in England: A Non-Scientific Survey." He published it in 1909 in four installments to challenge reader reactions which, not long delayed, were approving or disapproving strongly.

In 1910, the astute Jesuit editors of *America* capitalized on the stir this article had created by printing her bolder criticism: "What American Catholics Lack."[24] Louise did not spare the rod of chastisement: American churches were esthetic nightmares; cemeteries were atrociously pagan; money was overstressed; pews, too speedily vacated after mass. American Catholics had little private recollection and no interior life. The drama of the liturgy had been reduced to the dumb shows of private devotions. The "Hail Mary" had become "a drudge of work" for all occasions. Whereas the English priest remained "quite free of class and caste," at ease alike with squire or charwoman, the American pastors, too frequently, divided their attentions according to the social cleavage of the railroad tracks.

On the other hand, Guiney conceded that English Catholics lacked that free access to Protestant circles open to their American counterparts; and, contrary to a widespread supposition, she noted that the strength of twentieth-century English Catholicism derived more from converts than from either aristocratic old county families or new Irish immigrants. The handicaps of the Catholic writer, as a member of a subculture, applied to both English and American authors. In Louise's balanced assessment, these derived from limited talent rather than, as defensively alleged, from the obstacles of bias.[25]

## IV   *Priests and Priesthood*

If Louise's candor forfeited some popularity with Irish-Catholic readers back home, it neither strained her personal devotion to Catholic cultural tradition nor curtailed her friendship with Catholic clergymen. Between the leading American editors with whom she corresponded regularly and the British intellectuals frequenting her Oxford chambers, one might have compiled a "Catholic Who's Who." Catholics and intellectuals continued to consume a high proportion of her time and interests, and the former led her into a maze of pious research, combing ancient records for misty legendary figures like St. Frideswide, ninth-century princess-patron of the City of Oxford.[26]

Among the titles of her articles during this period, a selection suffices to attest her absorption: "The Shrine of St. Edward the Confessor" (*American Catholic Quarterly Review,* 1906); "Newman's Littlemore: A Few Addenda" (*Catholic World,* 1906); "St. Frideswide's Day in Oxford" (*Tablet,* 1907); "A Notable Collection of Relics for Oxford" (*Ecclesiastical Review,* 1907); "Elizabethan Catholics and [*sic*] their allegiance: some skirmishing thoughts" (*Catholic World,* 1908); "St. Bertram of Ilam" (*Catholic World,* 1910); "Epitaphs, Catholic and Catholic-Minded" (*Dublin Review,* 1913); "Newman Honored in Oxford" (*Ave Maria,* 1916); "Some Liturgical Origins in English Poetry" (*Ave Maria,* 1919); "Lent Satirized" (*Ava Maria,* 1920).[27]

As Louise's friendship with priests multiplied, in person and in correspondents, they prompted her to considerable composition also on the nature of their sacerdotal office. Her verse tribute to Father Arthur Day ("To One Who Would Not Spare Himself") was such,[28]

incomparably superior as a poem to the somewhat forced "To an Unknown Priest."[29] The essay "Flavian: A Clerical Portrait" did not fail to show her sincere admiration for the priesthood, but it suffered from overwriting.[30] "On the Loneliness of Priests," however, her best and longest essay in this vein, is still a classic pre-Vatican II conception of the dignity of the pastor and of his unique relationship to his flock. She compressed her theme into an opening quotation from Lionel Johnson's paraphrase of Plotinus: "Lonely unto the Lone I go;/Divine, to the Divinity." Her insights are tender; her respect, absolute. Without sentimentality, she focused on the priest's life of entailed sacrifice: "a demonstration which is all abstinence, a nearness without approach, an all-affectionate friendship which has dropped its personality upon the threshold . . . (to use a fine and abused word advisedly) the most romantic relationship under heaven." "Yet he lives along borderlands . . . . Long ago he faced that possibility, weighed the loss, took the leap, and chose in his youth a work like no other, as in its delight, so in its pain . . . . Cooperation of the most availing kind can never go so far as to cheat a priest of his sacred loneliness . . . . Since he will not shirk it, neither shall we."[31]

Nor was her promotion of priests confined to her poems and essays, though these were the best contributions within her means. Ceaselessly, she tried to secure their advantage in other ways. She introduced editor Heuser to the fiction of Monsignor Robert Hugh Benson and obtained serialization of Benson's *Mirror of Shalott* in *The American Ecclesiastical Review* (April-December, 1906).[32] She wangled an invitation from Father Gasson of Boston College for Father Arthur Day's needed rest in America.[33] She importuned the Reverend Henry Shandelle, S.J., to intercede with his Jesuit provincial for an English assignment for a brilliant contributor to *America* who could profit from exposure to Oxford.[34] All priests were her brothers, as hers was an unfailing sisterly solicitude for them.

## V   *Lionel Johnson*

Louise's feelings toward Lionel Johnson were certainly sisterly. Their natural kinship was evident in familial features that confirmed their origin from the same Muse: Anglo-Irish both, Catholic-humanist to the core, gentle and obscure. Interestingly, even their handwriting

and grammatical idiosyncrasies asserted the propinquity: "a slender, close slant, very odd, but not illegible; a true script of the old time, without a flaw" which seemed to whisper, "Behold in me the inveterate foe of haste and discourtesy, of typewriters, telegrams, and secretaries."[35] So, too, their common penchant for use of the colon, which each jocularly bemoaned to the other would be friendless after their demise.[36] When she had met Johnson in London in 1895, she had recorded that "He is not noticeably human . . . . But you know that I have a kindness for inhumanity."[37] Her affection ripened with acquaintance, and the mutual admiration never slackened. She dedicated *Robert Emmet* to Johnson, whose baronet grandfather had suppressed the Irish rebellion at New Ross in 1798; Johnson, who had previously acknowledged her as "the American poetess" in his 1896 *Chronicle* review of "Henry Vaughan, Silurist," dedicated his "*De Profundis*" to her in 1897.[38] She knew the rumored weakness for drink alleged to explain his periodic, and ever longer, withdrawals from London society; but she valued his patent virtue more.

When Johnson died suddenly in 1902 after a London street accident, she suffocated any personal judgment of his frailty in a single line: "In the bitter pathos of his end he was not with Keats, but with Poe." More to her point, however, she also noted that he had died, appropriately, on the feast of St. Francis of Assisi.[39] Her best memorial to his brief-breathing genius was her introduction to *Some Poems of Lionel Johnson, Newly Selected* (1912);[40] and her solid, if unsigned, contributions which she made in editing the *Catholic World* reprints of his articles (1910–1912)[41] and also Professor Thomas Whittemore's *Post-Liminium: Essays and Critical Papers by Lionel Johnson* (1911).[42]

Louise, a literary critic of integrity, as well as a loving friend, acknowledged that "The shortcomings of his verse lie in its Latin strictness and asceticism, somewhat repellent to any readers but those of his own [Classical] temper. Its emotional glow is a shade too moral, and it is only after a league of stately pacing that fancy is let go with a looser rein."[43] The poems which she selected represented a distillation of Johnson's best, compressed into fifty-plus pages: "Winchester," "Oxford," "In Falmouth Harbor," "The Dark Angel" (so like her own "Kings"), "By the Statue of King Charles at Charing Cross" (which, in its salute to "the fair and fatal king," could not

fail to evoke sympathy from Jacobite Louise), and Johnson's very last poem, perhaps the finest verse tribute from a student to his teacher, "Walter Pater."

Johnson's loyalty to persons, so like her own, extended also to his art, for it, too, was like hers: a nonprofessional concept of the man of letters; a disinclination to acknowledge work by signature; a sustained passion in vocation; a culture integrated beyond miscellaneous information; and a faith that was his treasure and an abiding peace and compensation. "At ten years old, or at the impossible sixty, he must equally have gone on, in a sort of beautiful vital stubbornness, being a unit, being himself."[44] Accordingly, Louise guarded his reputation protectively. As late as 1915, she was still fretting about the misplacement of Johnson's papers in the hands of Mr. Arthur Galton, who had neither published nor returned them since 1903.[45] Still later, hardly a year before her death, she forgot her own failing health to rejoice at the news that Robert Shafer of Annapolis had announced his forthcoming edition of Johnson's *Academy* essays: "The circle of Lionel's lovers is certainly growing, as it was bound to do!"[46] Christian humanists were precious because rare; and young bridge-builders, like Emmet and Johnson, were rarer.

## VI    Obiter Dicta

Louise's descent into the catacombs was not unrelieved, for she briefly enjoyed the personal resurrection brought about by a slender leaflet compiled by a Johnson-like admirer in the *Pathfinder*.[47] Edward J. O'Brien, in whom Guiney had discerned a resemblance to her "Lionel,"[48] had been actively engaged in honoring her own neglected achievement. His slight paper-covered tribute of 1911, prefaced by some verses of Clinton Scollard[49] "On the Lyrics of Louise Imogen Guiney," featured her familiar anthologized pieces: "The Kings," "The Knight Errant," "The Vigil-at-Arms," "Sanctuary," "To a Dog's Memory," and others. Sensitively, O'Brien's appreciation focused on the gaiety and faith which had made her "one of the few who go singing through the land." More importantly, it consolidated the devotion of O'Brien who, after Louise's death, collaborated perseveringly with Grace Guiney in editing Louise's masses of notes for belated posthumous edition of one volume of *Recusant Poets* in 1938.

Nor did Louise depend wholly upon others to establish her in the land of the living. Though now acclimated to the damp tunnels of the past, she emerged, periodically, to comment upon the contemporary scene. In two such poems, she touched sensitively upon problems still regarded as current in the 1970's: war and pollution. "Despotisms" protested, for example, the inane brutality of imperialist overreach in World War I:

> Lost on the wind is holy Belgia's cry,
>     And Poland's hope shrinks underground again,
> And France is singing to her wounds, where lie
>     The golden English heads like harvest grain.[50]

"The Motor," in retrospect, seems to anticipate the modern pollution of rampant technology:

> Vast intimate tyranny! Nature dispossessed
>     Helplessly hates thee, whose symbolic flare
> Lights up (with what reiterance unblest!)
>     Entrails of horror in a world thought fair.
> False God of pastime thou, vampire of rest,
>     Augur of what pollution, what despair?[51]

Greater than speculative reassurance that Louise's residual powers survived these years of blight is derived from "To An Ideal," originally published in *McClure's Magazine*.[52] It proves not only Louise's retention of poetic inspiration but her conversion of it to the service of her overriding concern with her search for God:

> That I have tracked you from afar, my crown
>     I call it and my height:
> All hail, O dear and difficult star! All hail,
>     O heart of light!
> No pleasure born of time for me,
> Who in you touch eternity.
> If I have found you where you are, I win my mortal fight.
>
> You flee the plain: I therefore choose summit
>     and solitude for mine,
> The high air where I cannot lose
>     our comradeship divine.
> More lovely here, to wakened blood,
> Sparse leaf and hesitating bud,
> Than gardens in the dewy vale for which the dryads pine.

> Spirit austere! lend aid: I walk along
>   inclement ridges too,
> Disowning toys of sense, to baulk my soul
>   of ends untrue.
> Because man's cry, by night and day,
> Cried not for God, I broke away.
> On, at your ruthless pace! I'll stalk a hill-top ghost with you.[53]

Louise had always been spiritually oriented, as evident in such early poems as "Summum Bonum" and "When on the Marge of Evening" (both written in 1892) and in "Sanctuary" and "Borderlands," written, respectively, in 1895 and 1896. The subsequent years of toil, disappointment, and refuge in Oxford as anchoress editor and scholar had purged her spirit of ambitions once fondly cherished; and, as a result, they had deepened her spirituality with a new sense of unchanging verities beyond the transiency of worldly praise. The period 1906–8, when she composed "Astraea" and "To An Ideal," reflects this religious maturity in a submerging of the self in submission to God in exchange for a new-found peace that was to sustain her, largely, through the years of trial ahead. In its frank communication of struggle partly won, "To An Ideal" expresses the paradoxical freedom found in resignation, avoiding alike the conventional constrictions of her favorite sonnet form and the imitations of Wordsworth and Tennyson that had shadowed her early verse. Unlike Francis Thompson who had pictured God as "The Hound of Heaven" relentlessly pursuing the fleeing soul, Louise identified herself as the hunter tracking the course, if falteringly, toward the Unchanging. Even so, she does not exult in a quarry caught as much as in a vision glimpsed from afar; for she conditions the goal (like Dante's light seen on the distant summit from the "Dark Wood" opening on the Inferno): "If I have found you where you are, I win my mortal flight." Her discovery is tentative, not terminal. For the fight for genuine fulfillment must still be carried to "inclement ridges" where only the humblest beauty can survive, purer there in its essential simplicity than in the opulent gardens cultivated in the lowlands.

One couplet of "To An Ideal" offers a personal explanation of her withdrawal from earlier preoccupations and former ambitions: "Because man's cry, by night and day,/Cried not for God, I broke away." And the last line bravely acknowledges the uncertainties

still to be met in the mystic's unending ascent, even after the dazzling epiphany of a flash of reassurance: "On, at your ruthless pace!/I'll stalk a hill-top ghost with you." The realism which closes the poem recalls the spirit of St. Theresa of Avila returning from a comparable transfiguration to the routine of supervising her Order's far-flung, and often turbulent, convents. That Louise, too, was not to dwell uninterruptedly on the heights of serenity or ecstasy is patent in the fact that soon, in 1910, she was to write one of her most disturbing poems, "The Kings," quoted above on pages 57–58. Here her vision evokes dark images of the Four Horsemen of the Apocalypse rather than of the exploding illumination of Dante's *Paradiso*. But this momentary relapse only authenticates "To An Ideal's" embodiment of the universal truth discoverable in every man's spiritual odyssey; whereas the earlier "Sanctuary" and "Borderlands" (quoted pages 99 and 100, respectively) give wider scope to the purely personal-subjective and, less chastened by experience, assume a permanence not truly to be found in the illusory security of momentary inspiration. There the victory is too easy. On the other hand, the diction of "To An Ideal," like life itself, conveys the agony inseparable from the mystic's ecstasy: "crown," "light," "hail," and "height" are juxtaposed against the austerer "track," "inclement," "ruthless," and "ridge." The same tension of opposites complicating the ceaseless struggle toward spiritual perfection expresses itself in the beckoning vision of the distant goal which she hails as "dear and difficult star." "Hill-top ghost" in the final line also sustains her appreciation of the unavoidable ambiguities confusing the quest for spiritual fulfillment. On one level of meaning it suggests her retreat from the secular mainstream; and, as coupled with God, it recognizes the fading of religion in her society. On another level of meaning the word "ghost" suggests the creative spirit "disowning toys of sense" for a liberation which releases the soul to ascend toward union with the eternal. As a Catholic, knowledgeable in pre-Vatican II theology and liturgy, Louise was quite familiar with this traditional equation of "ghost" with "spirit," particularly in the common usage of "Holy Ghost" as "Holy Spirit" or as "Creator Spirit." Whatever, the vision of "the glory and the dream" beheld "apparelled in celestial light" enabled her to persevere throughout the lonely, grinding years to follow.

# Last of the Recusants

THE final seven years of Louise Guiney's life guaranteed the "austerity" and the "inclement ridges, too." The pace, indeed, was ruthless: the dislocations plaguing England during the Great War; the bouts with illness, increasingly frequent and serious.[1] Throughout this period, she labored on her major scholarly work, *Recusant Poets.* Years before, in the jesting conclusion of a letter to Van Allen, she had written with ironic prophecy: "I am to be hanged, drawn and qu—no, only drawn, for a Copeland and Day Christmas catalogue; so, as I await the executioner, I send you my last words, and the assurance that I die fairly bookish and as 'recusant' as Campion of St. John's Oxford."[2] Her prophecy had all come true: Oxford, Campion, recusancy, martyrdom. By stepping aside from the mainstream, she had herself become the last of the recusants.

"Recusant" had been the term applied during the reign of Elizabeth to religious holdouts who repudiated subscription to the Act of 1559 by refusing to attend the Reformed Church services. Recusancy entailed devastating fines and civic disabilities that were intended to break the back of resistance to the union of church and state. More even than the disappropriation of church and monastic holdings, the Recusant Act consolidated Protestant conformity and the dissolution of the Old Faith. Priests who persisted in saying mass committed a capital offense, and they were penalized by barbarous torture and execution—for them, and for the laity harboring them. A few powerful noble families, buttressed by influence and royal blood, held out. Wealthy county gentry who persevered had their estates proscribed and, ultimately, confiscated. As always, the masses were the most helpless and the first forced to submit.

The indispensable doctrinal documents had been as thoroughly outlawed as their authors, printers, and owners. Printers who dared to circulate Catholic materials, however devotional (and, rarely, seditious by any extension of the charge), had their ears nailed to the public pillory. The law was draconically definite: "None shall bring

from beyond Sea, Print, Sell or buy any Popish Primers, Ladies Psalters, Manuals, Rosaries, . . . Legends or Lives of the Saints in what language soever they shall be Printed or Written, nor any Superstitious Books written in the English Tongue, on pain to Forfeit forty shillings for every such Book, to be divided as aforesaid." Spurred by this incentive, local justices of the peace, mayors, and bailiffs were licensed to search for "Popish Books and Reliques" and to deface and burn the evidence uncovered by their raids.[3] As a result, the Guiney-Bliss project was handicapped from the start; and the situation is accurately summarized in a letter from the Reverend John Hungerford Pollen, whose studies on Campion had enabled Louise to finish her biography of the martyred Jesuit: "The real truth is that the land is very bare. Catholic books were a danger in old times, and always seized in searches, which as you know, went on until after the '45. During the period of the best poetry . . . the searches and destructions were cruel. . . . I found one volume with hymns at Oxburgh [the ancestral home of Sir Henry Bedingfeld, 8th Baronet], and have not at all given up hopes of more elsewhere: but I fear that there cannot be much surviving in these places."[4] From the rolls of such recusants, Louise and her Jesuit collaborator, the Reverend Geoffrey Bliss, assembled the evidence of the strangled culture of Old England.

To do this research was exhausting. Bliss had extra-Oxford duties assigned that allowed him few weekends for exchange and conference,[5] and Louise had to interrupt her researches for the release of periodic, extraneous "potboilers" to sustain her throughout the project. Moreover, the penal laws against recusants had been so strictly enforced that many of the records had been consumed in public book burnings. A few manor attics still held the tattered, legally tainted documents; the libraries of England, even fewer. Yet, together, the collaborators accumulated an overwhelming testimony and, stubbornly, set about reducing it to a pattern. By 1915, *Notes and Queries* announced somewhat optimistically: "An earnest and confident appeal is made to readers of "N. & Q." to help a little towards the completion of a book lately compiled from out-of-the-way sources. It is called "The Recusant Poets," and covers, chronologically, the first two centuries of the penal laws against Roman Catholics. . . . We have gone pretty thoroughly over known ground, and covered a good many obscure or inedited old MSS., but should

be more than grateful to be told of others in private hands and not likely to have fallen in our way. . . . "[6]

By 1917, Louise reported to Van Allen, with understandable pride: "I have a book nearly ready, and the Oxford University Press will publish it when it can get its own staff back from Over There. I have done half of its very hard work, and an old friend, an S.J., Fr. Geoffrey Bliss, has done the other half. . . . The Recusant Poets: 1535–1745! Two fat volumes, too, with endless notes and bibliographies, and many a name of good lyrical standing which even you won't know."[7]

Grace Guiney, Louise's *fidus Achates* since 1911, jubilantly, if prematurely, also announced to the Frohocks, on September 26, 1920: "Cousin Lou had finished her BOOK!"[8] By then, Louise was a speechless invalid; for she had been stricken by arteriosclerosis on September 8 at Clytha Cottage, Abergavenny, Wales. Brought back to a friend's home in Oxford, she died within two months on November 2, 1920—on, fittingly, the Feast of All Souls;[9] and she was buried beside Aunt Betty in Wolvercote Cemetery, Chipping Campden. Vainly, Grace Guiney attempted to complete the project. In 1923, Father Bliss sadly returned the materials in his possession, unable to persevere longer. He confirmed the contents and status of the unedited notes in a letter to Mabel E. Tenison:

> The "biographies and bibliographical notes" form nearly half the work, and owe most of their value to Miss Guiney's wonderful knowledge of the byeways of late 16th and early 17th century history, Catholic and other. A great deal of material is from very scarce books or from unpublished sources, and will be new to all except a few students. The book would make two volumes; it contains much information—some quite new—on the history of the ancient Catholic families and many of the English Catholic martyrs.[10]

Fifteen years later—and eighteen after Louise's death—Grace Guiney, aided by Edward J. O'Brien who had compiled the *Pathfinder*'s Guiney tribute in 1911, succeeded in assembling one volume for publication. This Sheed and Ward edition of 1938 had been made possible by advance subscriptions raised by Dr. James A. Magner of Chicago.[11] The materials for a second volume remain unedited, but they are in the custody of Professor Thomas Birrell of Nijmegen University who still plans to complete the work begun by Grace Guiney and O'Brien.

The dates 1535–1745, setting the scope of Louise's plan for *Recusant Poets,* indicated her intention to begin with Thomas More (1478–1535) and to end with the Battle of Culloden, 1745. The plan would have covered the period from the first Tudor persecutions to the defeat of Bonnie Prince Charlie, after which all hopes of any Stuart restoration had been extinguished. The first, as released, covers only from Thomas More to Ben Jonson; and, as the editors explained, new bibliographical and textual knowledge appearing in the interval between Louise's death and 1938 required revision of several chapters, such as those on Thomas Lodge, Henry Constable, William Alabaster, and Ben Jonson.

Louise's criteria for admission to the anthology were strict: where selected contributors were converts, only in exceptional instances had verse from their pre-Catholic days been included; and such inclusions had to be supported by "spiritual foreshadowings plain in the extreme."[12] If a Jonson or an Alabaster relapsed in public profession of his creed, only the verified work of his Catholic period was used. Although some familiar lines win instant recognition (such as "Mortality, behold and fear" and "The glories of our birth and state"), many of the selections are undistinguished, for they lack any compelling literary artistry. Others, as Guiney duly noted, had become lyrical mainly by excision from longer narrative texts like "The Pilgrimage of Grace." The crushing onus of the penal laws militated against the freedom indispensable to creativity; as a result, the historical value of the collection outweighed its literary significance.

Louise was less interested in proving that Catholics were poets, or better poets because they were Catholic, than in showing not only the considerable number of Catholic authors who had continued to write despite the threat of punishment but also the distinctive features of their works as compared to Protestant contemporaries who were often superior from a purely literary standpoint:

It need be no surprise if the distinction between Catholic and Protestant religious poetry is not immediately obvious. The Reformers retained far more of Christian truth than they threw away. . . . The differences, however, are perceptible to a Catholic reader, be he never so great a lover of Herbert and Vaughan and Giles Fletcher. . . . and yet what worlds asunder, to take an extreme instance, are those two splendid poems, the Nativity Odes of Milton and Crashaw! In the first, a stately reverence, cold almost to forma-

lism; in the other simplicity, confiding tenderness, an abandon of delight, a reckless ardor and happy daring born of the sense that exaggeration is here impossible.[13]

Though often minor, literary quality was far from negligible. Surrey's sonnets are here; and Southwell's "A Child of My Choice," which Louise preferred to the better-known "Burning Babe." So is Thomas Lodge's "Of Rosalynde," bequeathed for reinvestment to William Shakespeare, just as Lord Vaux of Harrowden's "The Image of Death," included here, was to supply the original of the three stanzas spoken by the First Gravedigger in *Hamlet*. Side by side with Henry Howard, one finds that quaint man of letters, Nicholas Grimald, whose *Christus Redivivus* (possibly written in Cologne in 1543) became the direct ancestor of the Oberammergau Passion Play.[14]

With Louise's consistent sympathy for "the great meanings in minor things," she could not have overlooked the importance of recusant culture; for she had uncovered a treasure trove of social significance in the priest-holes of England. Historians, as well as literary scholars, remain in her debt whenever they reassess extraofficial records between 1535 and 1745. For she did much to reconstruct the underground life of England which persecuting governments and Whiggish apologists had buried when they could not extirpate it. Her study does not refute the record, so much as sets it in a fuller perspective allowing a clearer understanding of religious changes antecedent to the development of modern industrialism and capitalism. Where Max Weber, Richard Tawney, and Amintore Fanfani took the high road of economics to illumine the relationship of Protestantism to industrial capitalism, Louise, characteristically, took the low road of obscure singers.[15] What might have become an antiquarian's rummaging became an estimable insight, obliquely, into the spiritual and social history of Great Britain.

Although Louise, the born hero worshiper, took pride in the recusant record of independence in the face of oppression, she kept her sense of humor and light touch to the end. Some in her company of recusants were incongruously grotesque and were born to be martyred in any society. Myles Hogarde's doughty polemics, for example, she describes as "loud, verbose efficiency."[16] Jasper Heywood, a Jesuit priest and the son of John Heywood the epi-

grammatist, is spared neither his native contentiousness nor the predisposition to mental unbalance that clouded his last years after deportation to the Continent. Nor is *Recusant Poets* clerically dominated; much less is it a priest-ridden work. Long before the age of ecumenism and the emergence of the layman, she credited lay leadership with its influence in preserving the faith among the recusants: Francis Tregian, the wealthy landowner who impoverished himself in the care of refugees at home and abroad; Richard Verstegan, exiled printer and publisher.

Her exhaustive researches have already enriched scholars by a pathfinder's trail to neglected writers like Henry Constable and Sir Edward Sherburne. Her probes have provided thesis materials on the period for graduate students yet to come. Her style, in both introductory biographies and in footnotes even, evidences the unlost sparkle that, from the very start, had made her incapable of a bad phrase, though she might mar a sentence or two and miff a meter now and then. It makes one look forward to the issue of volume two of *Recusant Poets,* especially for her treatment of Dryden and Pope. Assuredly, her exhaustive researches enable us to understand the fitness of the inscription on her gravestone in Oxford: *DELAS-SATA* ("Worn-out").

## CHAPTER 13

# Summary

TO say that Louise Imogen Guiney's quietly heroic life was her masterpiece is not to disparage her works. Her thirty-two published books and hundreds of magazine contributions testify not only to her indefatigible productivity, but, in more cases than not, they evidence also her artistry and estimable scholarship. Her chevalier songs and her religious lyrics bear comparison with those of any American poet for their vigor and their unsaccharine spirituality. Her usual recourse to traditional verse forms, however, may have somewhat inhibited her freedom of self-expression; yet she infused even the popular conventions of her day with her unmistakable personality and, usually, with a superior rendition.

If one makes allowance for the girlish prolusions of the early *Goose-Quill Papers* (where her natural talent for the personal essay is already apparent), her informal essays meet the standards of the best which America has produced in this vein: always charming, once the early affectation has yielded to a more mature growth; amazingly varied in their miscellaneous, but controlled, erudition; intimate often as a private conversation; and gaily light without frivolity. Unfortunately, like the verse forms which she too readily accepted from a declining vogue, the essay, too, as a genre was already passé when she adopted it. Nevertheless, the best of *Patrins,* such as "Wilful Sadness in Literature" and "The Rabid *versus* the Harmless Scholar," are solidly rich in consistent adherence to humanistic critical principles, although her predilection for the past never blinded her to the emergence of new talent (Harold Frederic's, Gerard Manley Hopkins', or Aubrey Beardsley's, for example), which she was quick to perceive and to praise.

Her most enduring criticism, however, resides in her studies of Mérimée, Mangan, and Lionel Johnson, as the cream of her scholarship lies in her editions of lost Elizabethan and Caroline poets. Unlike *A Little English Gallery,* which was essentially an impressionistic appreciation of Vaughan, Hazlitt, and Dr. Johnson's circle, her editions of Thomas Stanley and of the recusant poets are

undergirded with exacting evaluations without forfeiting the alert appreciation or the generous enthusiasm which kept her quintessentially positive throughout a life of lonely hardship. Her journalism, often expedited by the pressures of making a living, was principally directed at explaining Englishmen and Americans to each other and, harder still, explaining Catholics to themselves.

But if *Recusant Poets* has enriched the social and cultural historians, as well as the literary critics, of England's shaping past, Louise's voluminous correspondence is valuable for its insights into the spirit and personages of her own day. Yet, while a mirror of her age, it vividly reflects her own image: animated, even sparkling through the shadows of the ellipses unavoidable in intimate exhange between personal friends. Fred Holland Day, recipient of so many letters from her, may not have been wholly wrong in guardedly hoarding this correspondence in the expectation that the future would ultimately acclaim Guiney as a unique exemplar of epistolary art.

In more than in her epistolary insights, Louise's life was a commentary upon her times. Without shirking involvement in the present, she had a rare sense of the past, wanting to the rapidly changing pace in America. In this awareness she shared something of Henry James's, Hawthorne's, and T. S. Eliot's perceptions. But as an expatriate to England after 1900 she was neither escapist nor hedonist. On the contrary, she sought to be a bridge-builder between Old and New Worlds whose respective virtues she represented equally.

In view of what she did, and who she was, it is dispiriting that Helen Howe's otherwise admirable *The Gentle Americans* (New York, 1965) covers Beacon Hill from Charles Street to Park Street without once referring to the scintillating Bostonian who had fascinated Holmes and the Fields, as well as impressed Miss Howe's own father-editor, Mark de Wolfe-Howe, when he had collaborated with Guiney in the 1880's and early 1890's. For, in the hour of Boston's waning lights, Louise's beacon had twinkled brightly from Pinckney Street.

It is sadder that the church which had profited from her cultured representation of Christian humanism during Catholicism's American adolescence used her and forgot her. Though unpolemical, Guiney was Christian to the core, risking ostracism from Yankee acceptance

by her steady witness to older traditions. She was ecumenist and saint before the former's modern species had recognizably evolved or before the latter's identification had been remotely associated with her kind of lay professionalism. No papal decoration was ever offered to her, although parish organists received medals for their pious fidelity, and although successful investment brokers were smothered in knighthoods. Holy Cross College has loyally maintained the Guiney Collection in its Dinand Memorial Library; but no college or university ever offered Miss Guiney an honorary degree during her lifetime, or conferred one on her posthumously. The metal of her mintage has been weighed too lightly; but, to her credit, her obscurity was largely self-elected. Her talents were spent reclaiming the deserts of bypassed merit. Today her turn has come to be remembered.

# Notes and References

*Chapter One*

1. *Goose-Quill Papers* (Boston, 1885), pp. 125–26.

2. *Ibid.,* p. 118. (Significantly, Lord Nelson was among her hoyden heroes.)

3. The Religious of the Sacred Heart of Jesus are now addressed as "Sisters." The school at Elmhurst was subsequently relocated in nearby Portsmouth, Rhode Island, and is now closed.

4. *Letters of Louise Imogen Guiney,* ed. Grace Guiney, 2 vols. (New York and London, 1926), I, 8. Hereafter *Letters.*

5. *Patrins* (Boston, 1897), p. 86.

6. "Beside Hazlitt's Grave," *Happy Ending* (Boston, 1927), p. 47.

7. "Writ in my Lord Clarendon his History of the Rebellion," *Happy Ending,* p. 117.

8. *Patrins,* pp. 29–31.

9. *Happy Ending,* p. 15.

10. "Despotisms, II. The War: 1915," *ibid.,* p. 183.

11. "To a Dog's Memory," *ibid.,* p. 14.

12. Nicholas John Loprete, "The Knight Errant: A Study of Heroism in the Works of Louise Imogen Guiney." (Unpublished M.A. thesis, Columbia University, 1956.)

13. Typescript copy, dated 1906, Van Allen correspondence, Guiney Room, Holy Cross College. Reverend W. H. van Allen, Episcopalian Rector of the Church of the Advent, Boston, was a life-long friend and confidant of Guiney.

14. Published unsigned in *McClure's,* May, 1910, as *"De Amore Amicorum."* Reprinted in *Happy Ending* p. 180.

15. *Letters,* I, 60.

16. E. M. Tenison, *Louise Imogen Guiney: Her Life and Works, 1861–1920* (London, 1923), p. 13.

17. English for *"Ad Majorem Dei Gloriam,"* motto of the Society of Jesus.

18. "Astraea," *Happy Ending,* p. 35.

19. *Ibid.,* p. 98.

20. "The Catholic Note in Contemporary Poetry," *America, XII* (December, 1914), 200–201.

21. Tenison, p. 9. Quoted from an interview with Miss Guiney by Boston journalist Mabel Aldrich, printed in *The Critic,* September 9, 1893.

22. "Memories of an Old Girl," written for the Elmhurst Alumnae Reunion, April, 1907. Holy Cross.

23. *Letters,* I, 2–3.

24. *Ibid.* p. 2.

25. *Songs at the Start* (Boston, 1884), pp. 38–40. Never included in subsequent Guiney collections.

26. See Chapter 4, p. 41, for President L. Clarke Seelye's inquiry of June 4, 1888. Also note 6, p. 138.

27. Clara M. and Rudolph Kirk, *William Dean Howells* (New York, 1962), p. 176.

28. Tenison, p. 60. Quoted from the *Evangelical Independent,* of which editor Dr. William Hayes Ward (1835–1916) was a close friend and patron of Guiney's during her brief career as Post-mistress of Auburndale.

### Chapter Two

1. See William L. Lucey, S.J., *"Louise Imogen Guiney and Her Songs at the Start," Records of the American Catholic Historical Society of Philadelphia,* Vol. 66 (March, 1955), pp. 53–63.

2. Rachel Norton, a Boston Jewess and her brother George, were Louise Guiney's oldest and closest friends. The Guiney-Norton letters which bridge the most conspicuous gap in the published Guiney correspondence were donated to Holy Cross College by the Nortons' niece, Miss Esther Lissner.

3. Mrs. Guiney's maiden name was Doyle.

4. Lucey, *op. cit.,* p. 57.

5. Included in *The White Sail and Other Poems* (Boston, 1887).

6. The one exception: "Spring," *Happy Ending* (revised, posthumous edition), p. 131.

7. Jacob Sheafe, an early Bostonian, laid to rest in 1658, in a northerly corner of King's Chapel Burying Ground, Tremont Street, Boston.

8. "Poete My Maister Chaucer."

### Chapter Three

1. "An English Literary Cousin," *Atlantic Monthly,* LIV (October, 1884), 467–77.

2. Grant, one of her heroes, especially for his courteous treatment of Lee, is described in the Ode as coming:

Mid trailing of arms, and drum-taps solemn
And rustle of lowering flags in the column,
From the psalm of the guns to the peace of God.

3. Guiney to Rachel Norton, October 2, 1885. Holy Cross.

4. Alice Brown, *Louise Imogen Guiney, A Study* (New York, 1921), p. 38. Miss Brown, prolific writer of the *fin de siècle,* was close friend and Beacon Hill neighbor of Guiney. Together they co-edited the *Pilgrim Scrip* and *A Summer in England,* collaborated on *Three Heroines of New England Romance, The Merrylinks,* and *Robert Louis Stevenson.* Together they toured England and Wales in 1895. After Guiney's death in 1920, Miss Brown burned the files of letters received by Guiney, acting on instructions left with her. See Reverend Francis Sweeney, S.J., "A Friend of Lou Guiney's," *America,* XXX (February 19, 1949), 546–47.

5. Guiney to Norton, July 19, 1884. Holy Cross.

6. Guiney to Mr. Miller, March 4, 1898. Cordon Collection of Guiney Letters. Holy Cross.

7. Guiney to Norton, January 8, 1885 and February [?], 1885. Holy Cross.

8. "The Romance of a Postman," *The Boston Sunday Budget* (January 8, 1882), pp. 5–6.

9. A. L. S. Guiney to Louise Chandler Moulton, March 2, 1885. Louise Chandler Moulton Papers, Library of Congress. Moulton, author of *June Clifford, This, That, and the Other,* and *Poems and Sonnets,* fashionable Bostonian of the 1880's and 1890's, was an early patron of Guiney. She entertained the day's *literati* in her salon on Rutland Square.

10. Autobiographical sketch, 1892. Typescript page. Curio cabinet, Guiney Room. Holy Cross.

11. *Letters, II,* 207. To Arthur K. Gibson, Cornwall, July 1, 1915.

12. *Poets and Pilgrims* (New York, 1925), p. 176.

13. Rachel Romano, "An Indexed Synthesis of the Critical Thought of Louise Imogen Guiney" (Unpublished M.A. thesis, De Paul University, 1957).

14. Mark De Wolfe Howe, *Memories of a Hostess* (Boston, 1922), p. 288. Annie Fields, always an admirer of Louise, listed her (if ineffectually) in her will. Sarah Orne Jewett was instrumental in placing Louise in the Boston Public Library.

15. "Tarpeia" was anthologized by Emma Elise West in *Werner's Readings and Recitations,* No. 22 (New York, 1899), 91–93.

16. "Four Books of Verse," *Atlantic Monthly,* LXI (March, 1888), 417.

## Chapter Four

1. The publishing firm of Copeland and Day was located on Corn Hill, Boston, in the center of the bookshops recently demolished by urban renewal projects of the 1960's. The firm published five Guiney titles. For its high standards in the 1890's, see *Publishers Weekly* (June 3, 1899), p. 920;

also, *ibid.* (March 21, 1942), pp. 1168–71. Herbert Copeland, Harvard graduate and art enthusiast, was partner of Miss Guiney's intimate friend and distant cousin, Fred Holland Day, whose story is related in Chapter 5, following.

2. Cram, a leader of the Gothic revival and vociferous medievalist, designed the Cathedral of St. John the Divine, New York. (Bertram Goodhue, another member of the circle, designed the Church of St. Thomas on Fifth Avenue.) Berenson, brilliant, if flighty, protégé of Mrs. Jack Gardner, became a distinguished authority on Renaissance art and was long resident in Florence. *The Knight Errant* (published in Boston, April, 1892–January, 1893) featured on its cover an image of the "knight errant" later celebrated in the lead poem of Guiney's *A Roadside Harp* (1893). Format and contents were in the spirit of William Morris and the Kelmscott Press. See Edna B. Titus, *Union List of Series in Libraries of the United States and Canada,* 3rd ed. (New York, 1965).

3. Medieval-monastic titles were part of the semijocular revivalist ritual observed by this blithe brotherhood of young intellectuals. *Letters,* I, 256–57. To Reverend W. H. van Allen, Auburndale, Mass., May 8, 1899.

4. Ralph Adams Cram, *My Life in Architecture* (New York, 1925), p. 30.

5. *Letters* I, 116. To Mrs. Herbert Clarke, Auburndale, Mass., June 24, 1896.

6. Reverend L. Clark Seelye, first president of Smith College, had written to Guiney from Northampton, Mass., June 4, 1888. (A.L.S. Holy Cross.) The secretary-signed response, also at Holy Cross, was dated June 9, 1888.

7. Frank Luther Mott, *A History of American Magazines,* 4 vols. (Cambridge, Mass., 1957), IV, 273.

8. *Ibid.,* III, 509.

9. *Ibid.,* p. 503; IV, 151.

10. Child invalid and neighbor.

11. Respectively, *Catholic World, XCV* (September, 1912), 753–69; and *ibid.,* LXXXIII (July, 1906), 447–55.

12. *Letters,* II, 247. Dated only 1919.

13. *Brownies and Bogles* (Boston, 1888), pp. 11–13.

14. *Ibid.,* pp. 159–74 *passim.*

15. *Letters,* II, 207. To A.K. Gibson, Cornwall, July 1, 1915.

16. *Ibid.,* I, 135. September 9, 1896.

17. *Ibid.,* II, 58–59 [n.d.]. Gwenllian Morgan, first woman to become lord mayor of Brecon, Wales, collaborated for years with Guiney on an ambitious Vaughan edition.

18. *Letters,* II, 170–71. To Mary Winefride Day, Oxford, December 14, 1910. See also, *ibid.,* pp. 254–55, letter to Reverend Geoffrey Bliss, S.J. (on

"that big Animal Question"); and letter to Reverend W. H. van Allen (December 30, 1909), among morroco-bound typescripts. Holy Cross.

19. *Patrins* (Boston, 1897), pp. 218–19.

20. N.B. sonnet-tribute to Brontë, *Happy Ending,* p. 135.

21. For Guiney-Parsons relationship, see Chapter 6.

22. Guiney never signed this poem. Unfounded ascription has been made to Elizabeth Barrett Browning; but she had died long before its circulation. Appearance in the Boston *Globe* (April 30, 1899) suggests, circumstantially, Guiney authorship, as form and content suggest it internally. Under a variant title, "The Walk," Reverend Michael Earls, S.J., submitted the poem to *America* (May 27, 1921) as Guiney's. He noted: "These verses, hitherto unpublished, were written for the S.S.P.P. (Saturday Society of Peripatetic Papists) which perigrinated afoot from Oxford to pre-Reformation churches." He also identified the source manuscript: "Among the manuscripts which came to me in collecting the letters of Miss Guiney, one in her well-known script and signed with her initials, came from a priest in a Western college. This devoted friend of the poet [former Oxonian and member of the S.S.P.P.] stated that Miss Guiney had written the poem for him." (Guiney Room, Holy Cross.) *The Holy Cross Alumnus,* VIII, 2 (November–December, 1933), 17, records that former librarian Irving McDonald resolved the controversy "by producing the manuscript."

23. *Happy Ending,* p. 5.

24. *Ibid.,* p. 16. Miss Guiney and Alice Brown were caught in a storm while crossing Salisbury Plain in 1895.

25. Alice Brown, *Louise Imogen Guiney* (New York, 1921), p. 54.

26. *Letters,* I, 134, September 11 [1896].

27. *Happy Ending,* p. 53.

28. *Ibid.,* p. 88.

29. I. "In Leinster," *Happy Ending,* p. 57; II. "In Ulster," *ibid.,* pp. 58–60.

### Chapter Five

1. *Letters,* I, 109. To Herbert E. Clarke, May 12, 1896. (Clarke, who corresponded regularly with Miss Guiney until his death in 1912, was an English critic and poet, author of *Storm-Drift* and *Poems and Sonnets.* They saw much of each other during her first residence in England, 1889–91.)

2. "On First Entering Westminster Abbey," *Happy Ending,* p. 159.

3. Number I. "On the Pre-Reformation Churches about Oxford," *Ibid.,* p. 150. (The original gift edition was circulated "With the compliments of Messrs. Copeland and Day.")

4. *Ibid.,* p. 166.

5. Clarke proved a good mentor, as well as guide. With Louise, he labored over revision of her Oxford sonnets.

6. Later printed as "Sir Walter Raleigh of Youghal in the County of Cork," *Atlantic Monthly*, LXVI (December, 1890), 779–86. (Dr. George Sigerson, poet and physician, was president of the Irish Literary Society. His poet-daughter Dora, also active in the Irish literary revival, married Clement K. Shorter, editor of the *Illustrated London News* and early Brontë biographer.)

7. *Letters*, I, 27–28. To Herbert E. Clarke, July 7, 1891.

8. See Guiney to Edward H. Clement, editor of the Boston *Transcript:* "I have always been sorry I wrote for The Post in 1889–91, instead of my ain old organ." (A.L.S., April 19, 1899, Holy Cross.)

9. *Letters*, I. 174. To Herbert E. Clarke, February 3, 1897.

10. *Ibid.*, p. 140. To Reverend William Van Allen, September 30, 1896.

11. "Some Impressions from the Tudor Exhibition," *Patrins*, p. 57.

12. "The Lights of London," *Happy Ending*, p. 164.

13. "Strikers in Hyde Park," *ibid.*, p. 162.

14. "A Porch in Belgravia," *ibid.*, p. 168.

15. "Beside Hazlitt's Grave," *ibid.*, p. 47.

16. *Happy Ending*, p. 77.

17. *Ibid.*, p. 170.

18. A remote kinship to Mrs. Guiney (née Doyle) led Day to refer to her as "Aunt Jenny." She often appears in his and Louise's letter references as "A. J." Abroad, they both exploited the relationship ("Carter cousins") to validate their constant public association to Victorian surveillance.

19. Louis Arthur Holman (1866–1939), amateur collector and print seller at Goodspeed's Bookshop, commenced his serious interest in Keats c. 1908.

20. Amy Lowell (1874–1925), prominent for her leadership in Imagist poetry and her unconventionality as a Boston blue blood. Houghton Mifflin published her *John Keats* in 1925. Balked by Day's congenital indecisiveness in her efforts to avail herself of the Fanny Brawne letters, the energetic Brahmin called him a "silly hypochondriac," (Letter of Amy Lowell to Ferris Greenslet, March 22, 1921. Quoted by Hyder Edward Rollins and Stephen Maxfield Parrish, *Keats and the Bostonians* [Cambridge, 1951], p. 26.) Miss Lowell eventually had her way.

21. Rollins-Parrish, *ibid.*, fully credit Guiney and Day with their role. "Nor in all America have four people [Guiney, Day, Lowell, Holman] done so much as they to foster study and appreciation of Keats." (Preface, p. v, *Keats and the Bostonians*.)

22. For her lecture before the Women's Press Club of Boston in March, 1891, on the relationship between Keats and Fanny Brawne, Guiney relied heavily on her article on "Fanny Brawne," published in *East and West*, May, 1890. The same, with its continuation of Masson's indictment of

"shallow-hearted Fanny" ("minx minxissima," in Louise's phrase), was the substance of another lecture before a ladies' literary circle in nearby Lynn, in March of the same year. Subsequently, she published an article on Keats: "John Keats (1795–1821)," *A Library of the World's Best Literature,* XXI (New York, 1897), 8497–8500.

23. On September 6, 1934, McColvin acknowledged the arrival of all the letters from the Day Collection.

24. See "Boston Letter," *The Critic,* XX (November 11, 1893), 309.

25. Letter to Louis Holman, September, 1933, written six weeks before Day's death. Quoted by Rollins-Parrish, p. 47, note 48. (Unless otherwise indicated, Guiney-Day correspondence references are to holdings in the Library of Congress, made with permission of the executrix, Miss Grace Guiney, Oxford, England.)

26. Louise had picked up the rumor from some remarks made by Clara Novello, the opera singer. See Rollins-Parrish, p. 5.

27. Guiney to Day. Postcard, dated Chichester, Thursday 9 P.M. [1890].

## Chapter Six

1. Guiney to Day. London, January 1, 1890.

2. Published by Alfred Mudge and Son, Boston, 1891.

3. *Letters.* I, 43. Guiney to Herbert E. Clarke, June 30, 1893.

4. "The Annals of a Vendéan," *Catholic World,* XLVII (May-June, 1888), 152–63 and 355–69. Articles' references essentially same as those of longer, but largely inaccessible, text of *Monsieur Henri.*

5. In memorabilia cabinet, Guiney Room, Holy Cross, dated 8/30 [1892?].

6. *Letters,* I, 42. Guiney to Mrs. Frederick Briggs, December 26, 1892. (Briggs, née Ada Langley, was a well-known actress of the period.)

7. *The Critic* (September 2, 1893), p. 157.

8. Homans had achieved local fame for her portrayal of "Little Lord Fauntleroy" at the Boston Museum.

9. *Letters,* II, 41. Guiney to Dora Sigerson. Dated 2 Ship Street, Oxford, August 5 [1901].

10. "The Annals of a Vendéan," p. 369.

11. *Ibid.,* p. 367.

12. *Ibid.,* pp. 367–68.

13. *Happy Ending,* pp. 3–4.

14. "The Annals of a Vendéan," p. 156.

15. Thomas Carlyle, *The French Revolution,* II (New York, 1893), 144.

16. *Happy Ending,* pp. 11–12.

17. "Memorial Sketch," *The Divine Comedy of Dante Aligheri,* Thomas Parsons, trans. (Boston, 1893), pp. xi–xiv.

18. *Patrins*, pp. 117–23.

19. *XLVIII*, 843–46.

20. "T. W. P., 1819–92," Happy Ending, p. 104.

21. *Letters*, II, 253. To Miss——. Undated, Grangeleigh, Amberley, Glos.

22. Happy Ending, pp. 85–86.

23. *Letters*, I, 56.

24. *Happy Ending*, p. 49; and, *ibid.*, p. 99, respectively. (The latter first printed in *England and Yesterday*, 1898.)

25. *Ibid.*, p. 91.

26. *Ibid.*, p. 79.

27. "Spring Nightfall," *A Roadside Harp* (Boston, 1893), p. 15. Not collected in *Happy Ending*. Similar references made hereafter to original publication.

28. "Athassel Abbey," *ibid.*, pp. 17–18.

29. *Happy Ending*, p. 87.

30. Charles E. L. Wingate, "Boston Letter," *The Critic*, XX (November 4, 1893), 290.

31. The verses appeared on January, 4, 1894. Wyer, a contributor to the Boston *Evening Transcript*, edited *Spun-Yarn from Old Nantucket* (Inquirer and Mirror Press, 1914).

32. A.L.S., dated October 24, 1893. Holy Cross. (Dr. Ward, Congregational minister and editor of the *Evangelical Independent*, had nominated Guiney for the office.)

33. *Letters*, I, 58. January 18, 1894.


*Chapter Seven*

1. *Letters*, I, 100. To Dora Sigerson, dated April 15, 1896; *ibid.*, p. 129, to Van Allen, September 9, 1896; and, *ibid.*, pp. 197–99, to Dr. Richard Garnett, August 23, 1897.

2. *Ibid.*, p. 64. To Garnett, [early 1895].

3. Quoted by Tenison, p. 60.

4. *Letters*, I, 66–67, April 5 [1895].

5. *A Little English Gallery* (New York, 1894).

6. "Martha Hilton," *Three Heroines of New England Romance* (Boston, 1894).

7. *The House of Life by Dante Gabriel Rossetti*, Louise Imogen Guiney, ed. Unsigned (Boston, 1894). Her prefatory note also unsigned.

8. In addition to the Church of St. Thomas, Goodhue also designed another renowned New York Gothic church, St. Bartholomew's.

9. Jacob Blanck, *Bibliography of American Literature*, III (New

Notes and References

143

Haven, 1959), 309, states that the original manuscript in Guiney's hand, together with a covering note to the publisher, is in the hands of Frederic G. Melcher. Guiney was often unassertive about her claim to recognition as co-editor or collaborator, as in the instance of her share of Alice Brown's *A Summer in England* and *Merrylinks,* and of Thomas Whittemore's edition of Lionel Johnson *(Post-Liminium),* besides numerous unsigned articles and poems.

10. Edmund H. Garrett supplied the appropriate illustrations for each of the sketches. He and Guiney made a perfect team, whose cooperation was classically repeated in their subsequent edition of Mérimée's *Carmen.*

11. Van Wyck Brooks, *New England: Indian Summer, 1865–1915* (New York, 1940), p. 324.

12. Guiney immersed herself thoroughly in all subjects treated; her treatment, however, was less impressionistic than scientific in its deliberate focus on essentials, set in illumining perspective.

13. *Patrins,* pp. 233–43.

14. *A Little English Gallery,* p. 42.

15. The lives of Beauclerk and Langton form one biography in *A Little English Gallery,* pp. 173–227.

16. *Ibid.,* p. 161.

17. *Ibid.,* p. 142.

18. *Ibid.,* p. 126.

19. *Ibid.,* p. 170.

20. *Catholic World,* LVIII (January, 1894), 489–505.

21. *Atlantic Monthly,* LXXIII (May, 1894), 681–92.

22. *Letters,* I, 84–85. Guiney to Bruce Porter, December 17, 1895.

23. *A Little English Gallery,* p. 251.

24. *Ibid.,* p. 236.

25. *Ibid.,* pp. 290–91.

26. *Ibid.,* p. 291.

27. *Ibid.,* p. 117.

28. *Letters,* I, 77–79. To Dr. Edmund Gosse, October 1, 1895.

29. *Ibid.,* pp. 102–3. To Edward A. Church, Auburndale, April 22, 1896.

30. *Ibid.,* p. 69. To Herbert E. Clarke, Salisbury, June 6 [1895]. See also, *ibid.,* Guiney to Mrs. F. H. Briggs, 28 Gower St., W.C., August 16, 1895.

31. *Ibid.,* p. 74. To Herbert E. Clarke, August 26, 1895.

32. *Ibid.,* p. 69. To Herbert E. Clarke, June 6 [1895].

33. *Letters,* II, 64. To Gwenllian E. F. Morgan, Oxford, October 9, 1902.

34. Her own admission. See *Letters,* I, 72–73. To Clarke, 28 Gower St., W.C., August 16, 1895.

35. *Letters,* I, 69. To Margaret Haskell, London, August 15, 1895. (Auburndale neighbor and mother of the little invalid of the same name.)

36. *Ibid.,* p. 71.

37. Hawthorne had made a similar suggestion in *Our Old Home,* I (Boston and New York, 1892), 84.

38. *Letters,* I, 69.

39. *Ibid.,* p. 79. To Dora Sigerson, Auburndale, Mass., October 24 1895.

40. Alice Brown, *Robert Louis Stevenson, A Study,* with a Prelude and a Postlude by Louise Imogen Guiney (Boston, 1895).

41. See *Letters,* I: to Bruce Porter (December 17, 1895), 84–86; *ibid.* (June 27, 1897), pp. 186–87; on Gelett Burgess, *ibid.* (to H. E. Clarke, July 5, 1897), pp. 187–86; and (to Clement Shorter, May 7, 1898), pp. 220–21. Porter and Burgess were prime movers in the brief, but brilliant, publication of *The Lark* in San Francisco; and advocates of a fitting Stevenson memorial there. Porter designed the memorial fountain which was dedicated in November, 1898.

42. See Guiney's self-critique of this "Prelude," *Letters,* I, 61 (to H. E. Clarke, January 8, 1895): "some stanzas in a measure perilously like that of the 'Ode to a Skylark,' of all things! . . . "

43. *Happy Ending,* p. 120.

44. *Letters,* I, 102–3. To Edward A. Church, April 22, 1896. See also, *ibid.,* p. 95: to Herbert E. Clarke, January 21, 1896.

45. Tenison, p. 305.

46. "On the Pre-Reformation Churches about Oxford," *Happy Ending,* pp. 150–51. (Number VI here. Sequence slightly different from original listing in *Nine Sonnets Written at Oxford.*)

47. "Number XII" in revised-expanded sequence in *Happy Ending,* p. 157.

## Chapter Eight

1. *Letters,* I, 182. To Clement Shorter, Auburndale, May 9, 1897.

2. *Supra,* p. 89, note 29.

3. *Carmen by Prosper Mérimée.* Translated from the French by Edmund H. Garrett, with a Memoir of the Author by Louise Imogen Guiney (Boston, 1896).

4. Quoted from Tenison, p. 312.

5. *Letters,* I, 157. To W. H. van Allen, Auburndale, November 28, 1896.

6. See sonnet to Stevenson, quoted *supra,* p. 75.

7. "Memoir," *Carmen,* pp. xxv–xvii, *passim.*

8. *Ibid.,* pp. ix–xi.

9. *Ibid.,* p. xxv.

10. See Guiney's "The Knight Errant," *Happy Ending,* pp. 11–12: "Shall help me wear with every scar/Honor at eventide."

11. "Memoir," *Carmen,* pp. xii–xiii.

12. *Ibid.,* pp. xviii–xxx, passim.

13. "James Clarence Mangan," *Atlantic Monthly,* LXVIII (November, 1891), 641–59.

14. Lamson Wolfe & Company (Boston and New York); John Lane (London).

15. *Letters,* I, 139–42. To W.H. Van Allen, September 30, 1896.

16. Tenison, p. 173.

17. *James Clarence Mangan,* p. 112.

18. *Ibid.,* pp. 1–6, *passim.*

19. *Ibid.,* pp. 21–22.

20. *Ibid.,* p. 62.

21. *Ibid.,* p. 107.

22. *Ibid.,* pp. 110–11.

23. *Patrins,* "To Which is Added an Inquirendo into the Wit & Other Good Parts of His Late Majesty King Charles The Second."

24. "On a Preference for Living in England", *Atlantic Monthly,* 99 (April, 1907), pp. 569–72.

25. *Patrins,* pp. 5–6.

26. *Ibid.,* pp. 6–9, passim.

27. *Ibid.,* p. 233.

28. *Ibid.,* p. 237.

29. Quoted by Guiney, *Patrins,* p. 236.

30. *Letters,* I, 84. To Herbert E. Clarke, Auburndale, November 26, 1895.

31. Volume 17 (January, 1899), 600–04.

32. *Letters,* II, 186–87. Dated Longwall Cottage, Oxford, April 19, 1912. (Reverend J. J. Burke, C.S.P., was Paulist editor of the *Catholic World.*)

33. "Ten Colloquies," *Happy Ending,* pp. 40–42. The two "Colloquies" quoted here appeared first among the "Four Colloquies" in *The Martyrs' Idyl and Shorter Poems* (Boston, 1900). See also *Letters,* I, 141–42. To W. H. Van Allen, September 30, 1896.

34. "A King of Shreds and Patches," *Catholic World,* XLV (February, 1887), 668–83.

35. *Letters,* I, 173. To Herbert E. Clarke, dated February 3, 1897. (See also, *ibid.,* the letter next following the Reverend W. H. Van Allen, especially pp. 175–76.)

36. *Letters,* II, 248–49. To Edward A. Church. Grangeleigh, Amberley, Glos, January 10, 1919.

37. "An Inquirendo," *Patrins,* p. 290.

38. *Ibid.,* p. 319.

39. *Ibid.,* pp. 306–7.

40. *Ibid.,* pp. 292–93.

41. *Letters,* I, 197–99. Auburndale, August 23, 1897. See also *ibid.,* p. 183, to Herbert E. Clarke (May 29, 1897) and, *supra,* note 1.

42. Miss Guiney had long shown a proclivity to deafness, marked by her tendency to cup her ear in her hand, inclining toward speakers as she listened. It was intensified by her illness after returning to Boston from England in 1909–10. In her last years, she avoided attending the theater for this reason.

43. *Letters,* I, 187–88.

44. *Ibid.,* pp. 192–93, dated July 27, 1897.


*Chapter Nine*


1. *Letters,* I, 202–3. To Reverend W. H. Van Allen. Ocean House, Port Clyde, Maine, September 29, 1897.

2. *Ibid.,* p. 230. To Van Allen. Five Islands, Maine, July 9, 1898.

3. A.L.S. To Fred Holland Day. Dated July 10, 1898. (Library of Congress).

4. "John Keats," *A Library of the World's Best Literature Ancient and Modern,* XXI (New York, 1897), 8497–8500.

5. *Letters,* I, 231. To W. H. Van Allen, Five Islands, Maine, July 9, 1898.

6. Typescript letter to Mrs. P. N. Gilman, dated 16 Pinckney St., Boston, November 18, 1899. (W. H. Van Allen letters, Holy Cross.)

7. *Letters,* I, 235. To Herbert E. Clarke. Five Islands, August 4, 1898.

8. *Ibid.,* pp. 233–34. To Dora Sigerson. Five Islands, August 4, 1898.

9. *Ibid.,* p. 238. To William L. Graves of Columbus, Ohio. September 20, 1898. (In response to his note of appreciation.)

10. "A Last Word on Shelley," *Happy Ending,* p. 185.

11. "Emily Brontë," *Happy Ending,* p. 135.

12. Tenison, p. 313.

13. *Ibid.,* pp. 81 and 313.

14. *Loc. cit.*

15. Reverend William L. Lucey, S.J., "We New Englanders . . . ," *Records of the American Catholic Historical Society of Philadelphia,* LXX (March-June, 1959), 58–64.

16. A.L.S. Dated August 21, 1899. Holy Cross (Guiney, like Alice Brown, had been among the contributors to *Youth's Companion* during Howe's editorship.)

17. For songs composed and lyricized by Guiney, see Jacob Blanck, *Bibliography of American Literature,* III (New Haven, 1959), 307, 312–13, and 316–17.

18. Mary Jane Kehoe, "About Louise Imogen Guiney," *More Books. The Bulletin of the Boston Public Library,* Published by the Trustees. Sixth Series. XIII, 1 (January, 1936), 15.

19. Minutes, May 18, 1900, Boston Public Library Trustees.

20. Savage, promising author of *First Poems* and *Fragments,* died prematurely in 1899. Louise had used her connections to promote his recognition. Undoubtedly, his sudden death expedited her resolution to resign from the library.

21. Number 240 Newbury Street was the home of her schoolmate Katherine Kinney, since become Mrs. William Gregory Macdonald. (The Macdonalds committed their townhouse to Guiney's use during their summer vacation.) Number 16 Pinckney was close to Fred Holland Day's apartment at number 9 and Alice Brown's at number 48.

22. Tenison, p. 94. Dated January, 1899.

23. *Letters,* II, 7. To Dora Sigerson. Autumn, 1899.

24. *Ibid.,* I, 251. Auburndale, March 3, 1899.

25. *The Martyrs' Idyl and Shorter Poems* (Boston, 1900).

26. *Letters,* I, 218, Auburndale, February 7, 1898; and, *ibid.,* p. 227, Auburndale, June 13, 1898.

27. *Happy Ending,* p. 134.

28. *Ibid.,* p. 98.

29. *Ibid.,* p. 137.

30. *The Confident Years: 1885–1915* (New York, 1952), p. 243.

31. For the account, see *Letters,* II, 1–2 and 5, respectively, to Edmund Gosse (June, 1899) and to H. E. Clarke (June 23, 1899).

32. *Letters,* I, 254–55. Dated Boston, May 5, 1899.

33. *Ibid.,* II, 7.

34. A.L.S. April 19, 1899. Holy Cross.

35. *Letters,* II, 15.

36. *Ibid.,* p. 27. To Mrs. A. D. Jordan. Dated Dartmouth, Devon, March 21, 1901. See also, *ibid.,* pp. 30–32, the letter to "Mother Jordan's" daughter Mary (former "B.P.L." colleague of Guiney's), dated March 31, 1901.

## Chapter Ten

1. Elizabeth Doyle was buried in Wolvercote Cemetery, Oxford, beneath a Celtic cross designed by Louise, who was buried beside her in 1920. The Latin inscription on the monument applies to both: *DELASSATA* ("Worn-out").

2. Failing to receive the Belgian scholarship, Ruth was enrolled in the Holy Child Convent School, Mayfield, England.

3. In 1903, Louise was elected to honorary membership in the National Literary Society of Dublin: *The Bulletin* (November 6, 1920), p. 2.

4. Rightly, if informally, she has been acknowledged as the coeditor. See Professor Whittemore's Latin dedication of *Post Liminium: Essays and Critical Papers of Lionel Johnson* (London, 1911). Characteristically, Guiney did not sign even her Preface, pp. vii–ix.

5. Professor Thomas Birrell of Nijmegen University, Holland, is currently preparing the edition of volume two.

6. A.L.S. Willa Cather to Guiney. February 16, 1909. Holy Cross ("[no verse received] passed from hand to hand with so much excitement and eagerness.").

7. A.L.S. Ferris Greenslet, editor of *Atlantic Monthly,* to Guiney. August 10, 1903. Holy Cross.

8. Cartwright is the subject of "Childhood in English Seventeenth-Century Poetry," *Catholic World,* LXXXIII (July, 1906), 447–55; Digby Dolben, who had something of the precocity of Chatterton and who, like him, died young, was featured in "Digby Dolben," *Catholic World,* XCV (September, 1912), 753–69.

9. "Gerard Hopkins: A Recovered Poet," *Month,* CXXXIII (March, 1919), 205–14. See also *Letters,* II, 239–40 and 251. (Both to Reverend Geoffrey Bliss, S.J.)

10. *"Les Enfants d'Édouard,"* one of the abortive plays translated in 1893. See, *supra,* Chapter 6, pp. 56.

11. *Letters,* I, 168. To Herbert E. Clarke. Auburndale, January 10, 1897.

12. *Ibid.,* II, 16–17. To H. E. Clarke. Dated 16 Pickney Street, Boston, May 9, 1900.

13. *Ibid.,* pp. 76–77. To Clement Shorter. Dated 57 S. John's Road, Oxford, April 7 [1903]. Saintsbury's three-volume edition, *Poets of the Caroline Period,* was published by Clarendon Press, Oxford, in 1905.

14. Charles Morgan's review of F. E. Hutchinson's *Henry Vaughan: A Life and Interpretation* London *Sunday Times* (March 16, 1947), p.3.

15. *Katherine Philips, "The Matchless Orinda"* (Cottingham near Hull, 1904), pp. 5–8, *passim.*

16. *"Guiney, Louise Imogen," Dictionary of National Biography,* VIII (1932), 43–44.

17. "Literary Spying," *Catholic World,* LXXXV (August, 1907), 580.

18. *Thomas Stanley: His Original Lyrics* (Hull, 1907), p. xvii. (Guiney's edition of Stanley was apparently ready as early as 1904. See *Letters,* II, 113. To Florence Warren, medievalist and one of first women students admitted to Oxford. Dated [?] 1904.)

19. *Letters,* II, 104–5. To Bertram Dobell. Dated 57 S. John's Road, Oxford, February 2, 1904. See also letters to Dobell, *ibid.,* pp. 106–8 and 110–12.

20. Tenison, pp. 323–24.

21. *Letters,* II, 106. To Bertram Dobell. Dated 57 S. John's Road, Oxford, February 2, 1904.

22. *Ibid.,* pp. 245–46. To Professor Charles Mills Gayley. Dated Grange-leigh, Amberley, Glos, December 12, 1918. (Explained in sending him her notes on Francis Beaumont for Gayley's research on the dramatist.)

23. *Letters,* II, 123–26. To Mary Winefride Day, mother of Reverend Arthur F. Day, S.J., Guiney's "pastor" at Oxford. Dated Boston: Corpus Christi, June 14, 1906.

24. Miss Whitney had aided Louise before, her "Ann Whitney Fund" having enabled Louise to go abroad in 1901 after severing ties at the Boston Public Library. The amount according to Jessie B. Rittenhouse, the well-known anthologist, was, perhaps, "Five Thousand Dollars." (Typescript letter. To Reverend Michael Earls, S.J. Dated January 23, 1934. Holy Cross.) Guiney showed her gratitude by dedicating *Happy Ending* to Miss Whitney.

25. *Atlantic Monthly,* XCIX (April, 1907), 569.

26. *Loc. cit.*

27. *Loc. cit.*

28. *Ibid.,* pp. 570–71.

29. *Ibid.,* p. 571.

30. *Letters,* II, 197. To Reverend Henry Shandelle, S.J. Dated Long-wall Cottage, Oxford, June 18, 1913.

31. *Ibid.,* p. 234. To Reverend A. F. Day, S.J. Dated Amberley, Gloucestershire, Easter Tuesday [April 2], 1918.

32. Anne Fremantle, "Four American Catholic Essayists," *Commonweal,* XLIX (December 10, 1948), 228.

33. Anglo-Saxon Christian princess and nun, foundress of Oxford City, A.D. 912. Her nunnery was on the site of Christ Church. Louise was eager to revive her cult.

34. *Letters,* II, 130–32. To Clement Shorter. Dated 6 Winchester Road, Oxford, March 16, 1907.

35. A.L.S. To Blanche Bigelow, January 13, 1909.

36. A.L.S. To Blanche Bigelow, May 28, 1909.

37. Now out of print. A second, enlarged edition of 1927 is also unavailable. As early as 1929, quoted at $27.50 per copy. Subsidiary rights sold in 1963 to University Microfilms, Ann Arbor, Michigan.

38. Black-edged memorial card, signed. Dated 42 Pinckney Street, March 30, 1910. Library of Congress.

39. *Letters,* II, 161. Dated Ashbourne, Derbyshire, June 16, 1910.

*Chapter Eleven*

1. "Donne as a Lost Catholic Poet" *The Month,* CXXXVI (July, 1920), 13–19.

2. *Robert Emmet: A Survey of His Rebellion and of His Romance* (London, 1904).

3. James Joyce, *A Portrait of the Artist As a Young Man* (New York, 1960), p. 203.

4. *Robert Emmet*, p. 92.

5. *Ibid.*, p. 103.

6. See *The Cornelian*, St. Leonard's-Mayfield Magazine (May, 1965), p. 53. (The letter to Wilfrid Meynell is included in *Letters*, II, 53–55.)

7. Her personal copy, so annotated, is in the Guiney Room at Holy Cross College. The epigraph is from Isaias, Ch. 49, verse 2.

8. *Hurrell Froude: Memoranda and Comments* (London, 1904), p. 1.

9. *Ibid.*, p. 228.

10. Fairbairn, prinicipal of Mansfield College, Oxford, had used the phrase in *Catholicism, Roman and Anglican* (London, 1899).

11. *Hurrell Froude*, p. 1.

12. Preface to *Hurrell Froude*, p. xiii.

13. A.L.S. Guiney to Moulton. December 5, 1905. Library of Congress.

14. *Happy Ending*, p. 113.

15. The letters abbreviate the original Latin motto: *"Ad Majorem Dei Gloriam."*

16 Campion (Blessed Edmund) had been beatified by Leo XIII on December 9, 1886. He was canonized by Pope Paul VI on October 25, 1970.

17. *Blessed Edmund Campion* (London and New York, 1908).

18. *Blessed Edmund Campion* (London, McDonald and Evans, 1908). The second edition was printed in 1914 by Burns, Oates and Washbourne of London. Benziger Brothers of New York had handled American publication of the 1908 edition.

19. This was Campion's only book published in English. It had been written hastily in 1570, while he was hiding near Dublin. In spite of Holinshed's badly mangled printing of 1577, its style shines through. Waugh's perception of its merits is expressed in his *Edmund Campion* (Boston, 1948), pp. 40–44.

20. Waugh, *Edmund Campion*, p. 43.

21. *Blessed Edmund Campion*, p. 177.

22. *Ibid.*, pp. 181–82.

23. William L. Lucey, S.J., "Louise Imogen Guiney and *The American Ecclesiastical Review,* CXXXVI, 6 (June, 1957), 368.

24. Vol. III, No. 15 (July 23, 1910), 379–80.

25. "On Catholic Writers and Their Handicaps," *Catholic World*, XC (November, 1909), 204–15.

26. "Saint Frideswide of Oxford: A Study of A Cultus." Four articles. *The Tablet*, CXIV (October 16, 1909), 603–05; (October 23, 1909), 643–45; (October 30, 1909), 683–85; (November 6, 1909), 123–25. See also her article.

"St. Frideswide's Day in Oxford, 1912," *The Tablet,* CXX (October 26, 1912), 651–52.

27. See Selected Bibliography for publishing data.

28. "To One Who would not Spare Himself," *Happy Ending,* p. 113.

29. "To an Unknown Priest", *The Dolphin,* III (January, 1903), 52–53.

30. "Flavian: A Clerical Portrait", *The American Ecclesiastical Review,* XLVII (July, 1912), 2–8.

31. "On the Loneliness of Priests," *Catholic World,* LXXXVII (May, 1908), 166–69, *passim.*

32. Lucey, *op. cit.,* p. 367.

33. *Letters,* II, 125–26. To Mary Winefride Day. Boston: Corpus Christi, June 14, 1906.

34. *Ibid.,* pp. 195–97. To Reverend Henry Shandelle, S.J., June 18, 1913. (The promising writer hopefully to benefit from reassignment was Reverend James J. Daly, S.J., literary editor of *America,* 1909–11.)

35. Introduction, *Some Poems of Lionel Johnson, Newly Selected* (London, 1912), p. 14.

36. *Letters,* II, 192, to Clement Shorter (Longwall, January 22, 1912); and, *ibid.,* pp. 210–11, to Reverend Geoffrey Bliss, S.J. (Cornwall, 1915).

37. *Ibid.,* I, 74. To H. E. Clarke. Dated 28 Gower Street., W.C., August 26, 1895.

38. Characteristically, Louise omitted the dedicated *"De Profundis"* from her own edition of Johnson's poems.

39. Introduction, *Some Poems of Lionel Johnson,* p. 19.

40. This Introduction had appeared as an obituary tribute two months after Johnson's death: "Of Lionel Johnson: 1867–1902," *Atlantic Monthly,* XC (December, 1902), 856–62.

41. Mostly from Johnson's contributions to the *Academy,* the *Anti-Jacobin,* and the *Daily Chronicle* ("the gold dust of L.J."), not the essays edited by Whittemore and Guiney for *Post-Liminium.* (See *Letters,* II, 205. To A. K. Gibson, of Grand Rapids, Michigan. Dated Longwall Cottage, Oxford, April 28, 1915.)

42. Typical of Guiney, her preface was unsigned. This modesty is sustained in references to the Johnson edition in: A.L.S.; to Reverend Michael Earls, S.J., March 1, 1911, Holy Cross; and *Letters,* II, 170; to Professor George H. Palmer, December 11, 1910.

43. Introduction, *Some Poems of Lionel Johnson,* p. 21.

44. *Ibid.,* p. 13.

45. See letter to A. K. Gibson, *supra,* note 41. (These materials were returned in 1923, by Frederick Manning, Galton's executor.)

46. *Letters,* II, 255. To A. K. Gibson. Dated Grangeleigh, Amberley, Glos, September 16, 1919.

47. Edward J. O'Brien, "The Poetry of Louise Imogen Guiney," *The*

*Pathfinder,* V, 5 (May, 1911), 2–16.

48. *Letters,* II, 187. To Reverend J. J. Burke, C.S.P. [editor of the *Catholic World*]. Dated Longwall Cottage, Oxford, April 19, 1912.

49. Clinton Scollard was the husband of Jessie Rittenhouse, Louise's friend and well-known editor of poetry anthologies.

50. *Happy Ending,* p. 183.

51. *Ibid.,* p. 182.

52. There entitled "To A Served Ideal." *McClure's* XXVIII (March, 1907), 534.

53. *Happy Ending,* pp. 51–52.


## Chapter Twelve

1. See *Letters,* II, 232. To Reverend Geoffrey Bliss. Dated 4 Church Walk December 4, 1917. For details of Guiney's illness (vascular lesions at the base of the brain, affecting her vision and hearing), see, *ibid.,* pp. 223–25 to Grace Guiney (early in 1917), as well as subsequent entries to p. 237, *"vale, fratercule, vale"* (to Bruce Porter, April 14, 1918).

2. *Letters,* I, 142. September 30, 1896.

3. Abstract of Penal Laws. Quoted by Tenison, p. 248.

4. Quoted by Tenison, pp. 248–49.

5. Father Bliss regularly stayed at a neighboring priory.

6. Series II, XX (October 16, 1915), 300.

7. Typescript letter. To Reverend W. H. Van Allen. December 10, 1918. Holy Cross.

8. A.L.S. To Mr. and Mrs. L. S. Frohock. September 26, 1920. Holy Cross.

9. Miss Guiney died in the home of Mrs. Mary Mills, the mother-in-law of Christopher Dawson, the eminent historian.

10. Tenison, p. 321.

11. Sheed and Ward released *Recusant Poets,* I, in England in 1938 and in America in 1939.

12. Introduction, *Recusant Poets,* p. 1.

13. *Ibid.,* pp. 4–5.

14. *Recusant Poets, p. 84.*

15. Max Weber, *The Protestant Ethic and the Spirit of Capitalism,* trans. by Talcott Parsons (London, 1930); R. H. Tawney, *Religion and the Rise of Capitalism* (London, 1926); Amintore Fanfani, *Catholicism, Protestantism, and Capitalism* (London, 1935).

16. *Recusant Poets,* p. 129.

# Selected Bibliography

PRIMARY SOURCES

The most complete collection of Louise Guiney's works, first editions, letters, and memorabilia is in the Guiney Room, Dinand Library, Holy Cross College, Worcester, Massachusetts—Mr. James M. Mahoney, curator. All Guiney books published during her lifetime are out of print.

For libraries holding original Guiney letters and manuscripts, consult Philip M. Hamer, *A Guide to Archives and Manuscripts in the United States* (Yale University Press, 1961). Hamer lists 3,100 pieces at Holy cross; 8 boxes at the Library of Congress (approximately 1,000 letters, mostly to F. H. Day and Louise Chandler Moulton, besides hundreds of photographs); 201 pieces at the Henry E. Huntington Library, San Marino, California; one box at the University of Notre Dame, South Bend, Indiana; and 55 pieces at the Boston Public Library. Smaller holdings are at Vassar, Wellesley, Immaculate Heart College (Los Angeles), and the Houghton Library, Harvard.

1. Poetry

*Songs at the Start.* Boston: Cupples, Upham and Company, 1884. (Houghton Mifflin and Company issued the unsold sheets under its imprint, 1895).

*The White Sail and Other Poems.* Boston: Ticknor and Company, 1887.

*A Roadside Harp.* Boston: Houghton Mifflin and Company, 1893.

*Nine Sonnets Written at Oxford.* Cambridge: University Press, 1895.

*England and Yesterday.* London: Grant Richards, 1898.

*The Martyrs' Idyl and Shorter Poems.* Boston: Houghton Mifflin and Company, 1900.

*Happy Ending.* Boston: Houghton Mifflin and Company. 1909; Rev., 1927.

2. Prose

*Goose-Quill Papers.* Boston: Roberts Brothers, 1885.

*Brownies and Bogles.* Boston: D. Lothrop Company, 1888.

*"Monsieur Henri": A Footnote to French History.* New York: Harper and Brothers, 1892.

*A Little English Gallery.* New York: Harper and Brothers, 1894.

*Lovers' St. Ruth's and Three Other Tales.* Boston: Copeland and Day, 1895.

*Patrins.* Boston: Copeland and Day, 1897. Reprinted, Boston: Small, Maynard and Company, 1901; London: David Nutt, 1901.

*Robert Emmet: A Survey of His Rebellion and of His Romance.* London: David Nutt, 1904.

*Blessed Edmund Campion.* London: Macdonald and Evans, 1908. Sec. ed., London: Burns, Oates and Washbourne, 1914.

*Recusant Poets,* I, ed. Grace Guiney and Edward J. O'Brien. London and New York: Sheed and Ward, 1938–39. (Volume II under preparation by Professor Thomas Birrell of Nijmegen University, Holland.)


3. Editions, Translations, Prefaces

*A Summer in England. A Handbook for the Use of American Women.* Prepared by the Women's English Rest Tour Association. Co-edited with Alice Brown. Boston: Alfred Mudge & Son, 1891.

*The Divine Comedy of Dante Alighieri Translated into English Verse* by Thomas William Parsons. Preface by Charles Eliot Norton. Memorial Sketch by Louise Imogen Guiney. Boston: Houghton Mifilin and Company, 1893.

"Martha Hilton," in *Three Heroines of New England Romance.* Boston: Little, Brown and Company, 1894.

*The House of Life by Dante Gabriel Rossetti. Being Now for the First Time Given in its Full Text.* Prefatory note, unsigned, by Louise Imogen Guiney. Boston: Copeland and Day, 1894.

Brown, Alice, *Robert Louis Stevenson.* Prelude and Postlude by Louise Imogen Guiney. Boston: Copeland and Day, 1895.

*Carmen.* Trans. from the French of Prosper Mérimée by Edmund Garrett. Preface by Louise Imogen Guiney. Boston: Little, Brown and Company, 1896.

*James Clarence Mangan: His Selected Poems,* ed., with introduction, by Louise Imogen Guiney. Boston: Lamson Wolffe and Company, 1897.

*The Secret of Fougereuse,* trans. from the French of Louise Morvan by Louise Imogen Guiney. Boston: Marlier, Callanan and Company, 1898.

*The Sermon to the Birds and the Wolf of Gubbio. Being Part of the XVI Chapter and the Entire XXI Chapter of the Fioretti di San Francesco.* Privately printed for the translator, Louise Imogen Guiney. Boston: Copeland and Day, Christmas, 1898.

*Sohrab and Rustum and Other Poems by Mathew Arnold.* Biographical Sketch and Notes by Louise Imogen Guiney. Boston: Houghton, Mifflin and Company, 1899.

*The Mount of Olives and Primitive Holiness by Henry Vaughan,* ed. Louise Imogen Guiney. London: Henry Frowde, Oxford, 1902.

*Hurrell Froude: Memoranda and Comments,* ed. Louise Imogen Guiney. London: Methuen and Company, 1904.

*Katherine Philips, "The Matchless Orinda,"* ed. with Introduction, by Louise Imogen Guiney. Hull: J. R. Tutin, 1904.

*Thomas Stanley,* ed. Louise Imogen Guiney. Hull: J. R. Tutin, 1907.

*Post-Liminium: Essays and Critical Papers by Lionel Johnson,* ed., Thomas Whittemore, in collaboration with Louise Imogen Guiney. London: Elkin Matthews, 1912.

*Some Poems of Lionel Johnson, Newly Selected,* ed., with Introduction, by Louise Imogen Guiney. London: Elkin Matthews, 1912.


4.   Unpublished Works
"Henry Vaughan, Silurist."
"A Forgotten Poet, William Alabaster."
"St. Frideswide, Princess and Nun."
"William Hazlitt."
"John Donne."


5.  Selected Periodical Contributions: Prose (From the Guiney Collection at Holy Cross College, compiled in collaboration with William L. Lucey, S.J.)

*America*
"Questions of the Day: What American Catholics Lack," III (July 23, 1910), 379–80.
"The Pre-Reformation Churches in England: A Mood," IV (December 3, 1910).

*American Catholic Quarterly Review*
"Shrine of St. Edward the Confessor," XXXI (July, 1906), 513–31.

*Atlantic Monthly*
"An English Literary Cousin," LIV (October, 1884), 467–77.
"A Tory Parson," LIX (April, 1887), 524–32. A study of Mather Byles.
"The Water-Ways of Portsmouth," LX (July, 1887), 9–22.
"Sir Walter Raleigh of Youghal in the County of Cork," LXVI (December, 1890), 779–86.
"James Clarence Mangan," LXVIII (November, 1891), 641–59.
"Henry Vaughan the Silurist," LXXIII (May, 1894), 681–92.
Of Lionel Johnson: 1867–1902," XC (December, 1902), 856–62.
"On a Preference for Living in England," XCIX (April, 1907), 569–72.
"Hesternus to His Publisher," CII (September, 1908), 427–29.

*Ave Maria*

> "Catholic England as It Looks to an American," LXVIII (January 2, 1909), 12–15; (January 9, 1909), 42–46; (January 16, 1909), 74–77; (January 23, 1909), 107–11.
> "The Local Bad Man," LXXV (October 5, 1912), 426–30.
> "A Letter from Canterbury to an Invalid at Home," LXXVI (January 18, 1913), 65–69.
> "The Monster of the Highways," LXXVII (August 16, 1913), 207–9.
> "The Bodleian Library," LXXVII (October 18, 1913), 494–97.
> "Lastingham," LXXVIII (February 14, 1914), 200–201; (February 21, 1914), 240–43.
> "A Forgotten Confession" [n.s.], II (August 21, 1915), 244.
> "Newman Honored in Oxford," III [n.s.], (June 24, 1916), 818–19.
> "Our Lady of Noon," by Paul Claudel; translated by L. I. G., VII [n.s.], (February 2, 1918), 129.
> "No Empty Cradle," VII [n.s.], (June 15, 1918), 751–58.
> "Translators' Poetry and Translators' Prose," VIII [n.s.], (Sept. 7, 1918), 305–6.
> "A Lost and Recovered Poet," IX [n.s.], (April 5, 1919), 433–35.
> "Some Liturgical Origins in English Poetry," X [n.s.], (July 19, 1919), 65–68.
> "Lent Satirized," XI [n.s.] (March 13, 1920), 336–37.
> "Gleams of the Wisdom of Catwg," XI [n.s.], (June 5, 1920), 724–25.

*Blackwood's Magazine*

> "Some Account of Arcady," CXCIV (August, 1913), 266–74.

*The Book Buyer, A Review and Record of Current Literature.*

> "Harold Frederic: A Half-Length Sketch From the Life," XVII (January, 1899), 600–604.

*Boston Sunday Budget*

> "The Romance of a Postman," by Alicujusdam, "Budget Prize Stories" (January 8, 1882).

*The Catholic Encyclopedia,* ed. C. G. Herbermann, E. A. Pace *et al.,* 15 vols. (New York, Appleton, 1907–12).

> Contributed the articles on:
>> Chaucer, Geoffrey, III, 642–45.
>> Edmund Campion, Blessed, V, 293–94.
>> Guiney, Patrick Robert, VII, 72.
>> Johnson, Lionel Pigot, XVI, 47d.

*Catholic World*

> "A King of Shreds and Patches," XLV (February, 1887), 668–83.

"The Annals of a Vendéan," XLVII (May, 1888), 152–63; (June, 1888), 355–69.

"Reminiscences of a Fine Gentleman," XLIX (August, 1889), 612–16.

"William Hazlitt: A Character Study," LVIII (January, 1894), 489–505.

"Aubrey Beardsley: A Reconstruction," LXIX (May, 1899), 201–13.

"On Halos," LXXX (December, 1904), 294–99.

"Childhood in English Seventeenth-Century Poetry," LXXXIII (July, 1906), 447–55.

"Newman's Littlemore: A Few Addenda," LXXXIII (September, 1906), 820–28.

"Literary Spying," LXXXV (August, 1907), 577–80.

"On the Loneliness of Priests," LXXXVII (May, 1908), 166–69.

"Elizabethan Catholics and Their Allegiance: Some Skirmishing Thoughts," LXXXVII (August, 1908), 577–94.

"On Catholic Writers and Their Handicaps," XC (November, 1909), 204–15.

"Saint Bertram of Ilam," XCII (October, 1910), 23–36.

"Lilium Auratum," XCIII (June, 1911), 310–27.

"Lovelace and Vaughan: A Speculation," XCV (August, 1912), 646–55.

"Digby Dolben," XCV (September, 1912), 753–69.

"The Mock Chatterton," A study of Thomas Dermody (1775–1802), XCVII (April, 1913), 16–44.

"The Lavington of Manning," XCVII (August, 1913), 587–93.

"The Amateur Bargee," XCVII (September, 1913), 769–79.


*The Chap-Book*

"Trilby, I" (August 15, 1894), 157–60.


*Donahoe's Magazine*

"Lady Anne Fitzgerald and the Emmet Revolutionary Movement," LI (February, 1904), 117–20.


*The Dublin Review*

"Epitaphs, Catholic and 'Catholic-Minded,'" CLII (April, 1913), 254–68.

"Cromwell's Nickname: 'The Brewer,'" CLIV (April, 1914), 247–71.


*The Ecclesiastical Review*

"A Notable Collection of Relics for Oxford," XXXVII (October, 1907), 388–400.

"Flavian: A Clerical Portrait," XLVII (July, 1912), 2–8.

*Harper's Weekly*
  "'Arry and 'Arriet in Love," XLVIII (August 20, 1904), 1291.
  "Oxon versus Cantab," XLVIII (October 15, 1904), 1574–76.

*Holy Cross Purple*
  "General Guiney," III (June, 1896), 37–43.

*The Knight Errant*
  "A Note on George Wither," I (January, 1893), 98–103.

*Lippincott's Monthly Magazine*
  "Bed," XL (August, 1887), 271–76.

*Macmillan's Magazine*
  "Dr. Johnson's Favorites," LIX (January, 1889), 185–93.

*The Month*
  "Of Lionel Johnson: 1867–1902," By One Who Knew Him. LXXI
    [n.s.] (November, 1902), 460–69.
  "The White King," LXXIV [n.s.] (July, 1911), 33–39.
  "Incorporeall Souldiers," CXXVI (December, 1915), 610–14.
  "Anthony Munday," CXXVIII (July, 1916), 14–19.
  "An Oxford Private: Arthur Brandreth, M.A.," CXXIX (February,
    1917), 129–32.
  "Gerard Hopkins: A Recovered Poet," CXXXIII (March, 1919),
    205–14.
  "Donne as a Lost Catholic Poet," CXXXVI (July, 1920), 13–19.

*The Nation*
  "Henry Vaughan Unpublished Letters, With a Commentary,"
    C (March 11, 1915), Part I, 275–78.
    C (March 18, 1915), Part II, 300–03.
  "A Lyric Miracle," CI (September 16, 1915), 358.

*Notes and Queries, A Medium of Communication*
  "References Wanted," under *Queries,* Ninth Series, XII (July 26,
    1902), 67.
  "A Gallant Captain," under *Queries,* Ninth Series, XII (December 26,
    1903), 506.
  "Dr. Hall," under *Queries,* Tenth Series, I (April 2, 1904), 268.
  "St. Ia," under *Queries,* Tenth Series, IX (June 6, 1908), 448.
  "Shakespeare and 'Warray': Sonnet CXLVI," under *Notes,*
    Eleventh Series, IV (July 29, 1911), 84–85.

"To digg the Dust Enclosed Heare," under *Notes,* Eleventh Series, VI (August 17, 1912), 126.

"Quaritch MSS.," under *Queries,* Eleventh Series, VIII (September 13, 1913), 207–8.

"Redcoats," under *Notes,* Eleventh Series, VIII (September 20, 1913), 226.

"Hall Family, Friends of Strafford," under *Queries,* Eleventh Series, VIII (November 22, 1913), 409.

"The Recusant poets," under *Queries,* Eleventh Series, XII (October 16, 1915), 300.

*The Pathfinder*
"Lionel Johnson, 1867–1902," V, No. 2 (February, 1911), 11–16.

*The Quarterly Review*
"Milton and Vaughan," CCXX (April, 1914), 353–64.

*Scribner's Magazine*
"English Reserve," XXXIX (June, 1906), 757–79.

"English Weather," XLII (November, 1907), 630–32.

"Brother" (an essay on her favorite dog), XLVI (July, 1909), 116.

"The Point of View," XLIX (January, 1911), 121–24.

*The Tablet*
"Saint Frideswide of Oxford: A Study of a Cultus," Four articles, CXIV (October 16, 23, 30, November 6, 1909), 603–5.

"S. Frideswide's Day in Oxford, 1912," CXX (October 26, 1912), 651–52.

*The Universe*
"'Improper Editing'—A Counter Thrust," 362 (March 28, 1919), 4.

*Wide Awake*
"Fairy Folk," illustrated, XVIII (May, 1884), 364–65.

"Fairy Folk All," illustrated, XXIV (December, 1886), 21–23; (January, 1887), 121–23; (February, 1887), 167–70; (March, 1887), 243–47; (April, 1887), 306–10; (May, 1887), 386–90; XXV (June, 1887), 49–52; (July, 1887), 123–26; (August, 1887), 184–86; (September, 1887), 235–37; (October, 1887), 315–18; (November, 1887), 387–90.

"A New Fact About Captain John Smith" in "The Contributors and the Children," XXIV (December, 1886), 149.

"What Fancy Is," in "The Contributors and the Children," XXIV (February, 1886), 214.

"A Brave Girl," under "The Contributors and the Children," XXIV (April, 1886), 344.

"Sir Philip Sidney," in "The Contributors and the Children," XXV (September, 1887), 264.

"Enough's A Feast," "A Soldier's Answer," "Preventing Beauty," in "The Contributors and the Children," XXVI (December, 1887), 277, 342, 406.

"The Bluecoat School," XXXVI (December, 1892), 13–17.

"Hartley Coleridge, Ten Years Old," XXXVI (May, 1893), 544–47.

6. Verse Contributions: Periodicals and Anthologies

The most complete listing of Guiney verse contributions is in the card index of the Guiney Room at Holy Cross College. Sister Mary Adorita Hart's bibliography in *Soul Ordained to Fail* (Pageant Press, 1962), pp. 173–74, furnishes a useful, if limited, list of contributions to periodicals. Jacob Nathaniel Blanck's *Bibliography of American Literature,* III (New Haven, Yale University Press, 1959), provides under Reprints (pp. 316–18) a list of anthologies featuring Guiney contributions.

7. Letters

*Letters of Louise Imogen Guiney* 2 vols Ed. Grace C. Guiney. Preface by Agnes Repplier. New York and London: Harper & Brothers, 1926. Indispensable for insight into vibrant personality and range of interests and activities. Gaps in early life. Lacks index.

SECONDARY SOURCES

1. Biographies and Biographical Sketches

ALEXANDER, CALVERT. *The Catholic Literary Revival.* Milwaukee: Bruce, 1935. Good summary of Guiney's life and achievement; concludes that Guiney's rejection of America for England occasioned a setback of twenty years for the advancement of American Catholic letters.

BROOKS, VAN WYCK. *New England: Indian Summer, 1865–1915.* New York: Dutton, 1940. *The Confident Years, 1885–1915.* New York: Dutton, 1952. Both provide indexes of Guiney references setting her in perspective among her American contemporaries.

BROWN, ALICE. *Louise Imogen Guiney, A Study.* New York: Macmillan, 1921. Makes no attempt at conventional, chronological treatment. Impressionistic, but valuable for the recollections and appreciations of a close friend and collaborator.

*Dictionary of American Biography.* New York: Scribner's 1932. George

Harvey Genzmer's appreciation in Vol. VIII (43–44) is still pertinent for coverage and insights.

HART, SISTER MARY ADORITA. *Soul Ordained to Fail.* Pageant Press, 1962. Useful, if incomplete, list of verse contributions to periodicals.

HOWE, MARK DE WOLFE. *Memories of a Hostess: a Chronicle of Eminent Friendships Drawn Chiefly from the Diaries of Mrs. James T. Fields.* Boston: Atlantic Monthly Press, 1922. Glimpse of Guiney in association with Annie Fields and Sarah Orne Jewett.

*The New Catholic Encyclopedia.* New York: McGraw-Hill, 1967. Henry George Fairbanks' sketch in Vol. VI (856) is most current.

ROLLINS, HYDER EDWARD and PARRISH, STEPHEN MAXFIELD. *Keats and the Bostonians.* Cambridge: Harvard University Press, 1951. Fullest and liveliest treatment of Guiney's leadership in restoring appreciation of John Keats. Makes extensive use of Guiney-Day letters now in the Houghton Library at Harvard.

TENISON, EVA MABEL. *Louise Imogen Guiney: Her Life and Works.* London: Macmillan, 1923. Contains a useful "descriptive" bibliography. Text of biography, although warmly *sympatico,* somewhat effusively apologetic and confusingly organized. Source citations deficient.

2. Articles and Theses

BERRIGAN, DANIEL J. "Forgotten Splendor," *America,* LXX (March 4, 1944), pp. 605–6. A poet's criticism. Stresses the "positive" note in Guiney compared to the negativism in Millay; the discipline in Guiney, compared to the flashing perceptions of Dickinson—while equal in intensity to both.

BRÉGY, KATHERINE. "The Catholic Note in Contemporary Poetry, IV: Louise Imogen Guiney," *America,* XII (December 5, 1914), 200–201. Calls Guiney a "Valkyrie turned Crusader."

FREMANTLE, ANNE. "Four American Catholic Essayists," *The Commonweal,* XLIX (December 10, 1948), 225–28. Guiney listed with Brownson, Hecker, O'Reilly. Like Brégy (above), stresses the "violence" and "outsize-ness" of Guiney; but also attributes to her "the quintessential culture distilled by Agnes Repplier."

KURTH, PAULA. "The Sonnets of Louise Imogen Guiney," *America,* XLIII (August 9, 1930), pp. 430–31. Notes the prevalence of this form in Guiney's verse, especially its Petrarchan mode, and the recurrence of the past as dominant subject matter.

LOPRETE, NICHOLAS JOHN. "The Knight Errant: A Study of Heroism in the Works of Louise Imogen Guiney." Unpublished M.A. thesis.

Columbia University, 1956. Focuses on father-daughter relationship and its formative influence in shaping Guiney's views.

LUCEY, WILLIAM L. "Louise Imogen Guiney and Her 'Songs at the Start,'" *Records of the American Catholic Historical Society,* LXVI (March, 1955), 53–63. Establishes Guiney's appearance in print three years earlier (1880) than previously assumed. Especially valuable for filling in early gaps of the published *Letters.*

." 'We New Englanders . . .' Letters of Sarah Orne Jewett to Louise Imogen Guiney," *Records of the American Catholic Historical Society of Philadelphia,* LXX (March–June, 1959), 58–64. A common profession and love of Ireland bound the two authors. Letters quoted especially useful for showing Jewett's influence in placing Guiney in the Boston Public Library.

. "Louise Imogen Guiney and *The American Ecclesiastical Review,*" *The American Ecclesiastical Review,* CXXXVI, 6 (June, 1957), 364–70. Besides revealing account of Guiney's relations with American Catholic editors, shows Guiney's critical-progressive Catholicism. Traditionalist, but anti-formalist.

MONROE, HARRIET. "Two Poets Have Died," *Poetry: A Magazine of Verse,* XVII (January, 1921), 208–12. In parallel treatment with John Reed, Monroe repeats the common observation of Guiney's "fighting spirit." Notes also "the flavor of the nineties" in Guiney's poetry, making much of it look dated even by the 1920s.

ROMANO, RACHEL. "An Indexed Synthesis of the Critical Thought of Louise Imogen Guiney." Unpublished M.A. thesis. De Paul University, Chicago, 1957. Shows consistency of Guiney's critical principles from earliest to latest works. Somewhat narrowly literary in focus.


3. Bibliographies


BLANCK, JACOB NATHANIEL. *Bibliography of American Literature,* III, 305–18. New Haven: Yale University Press, 1959. Fullest and best of printed bibliographies.

Card index in Guiney Room, Holy Cross College, most complete in particulars.

See also, above, bibliographies in biographies by Tenison and Hart.

# Index